To My Friends, Neighbors, and Relatives:

FORGIVE ME

for waiting so long to tell you this

DAVID KIRKWOOD

ETHNOS PRESS
Pittsburgh, Pennsylvania

Forgive Me for Waiting so Long to Tell You This
First Printing: June, 1991
Copyright © 1990 by David Kirkwood

Unless otherwise noted, all Scripture quotations are from the *New American Standard Bible*. Copyright © 1960, 1962, 1963, 1968, 1971, 1972, 1973, 1975, 1977 by the Lockman Foundation. Used by permission.

Cover design: Tony Condello

Printed in the United States of America
International Standard Book Number: 0-9629625-0-3

To seekers everywhere

Acknowledgements

My sincere thanks to Ruth Kohl, Tony Condello, Virginia Steppling, LaVerne Kirkwood, Wayne and Addie Stidham, Val Cindric, Dr. Jack Stepp, Jim Flynn, Thom and Cathy Hickling, and Chris Manos for their help in the preparation of this book. Most of all, I thank my wife Becky, my daughter Charity, and my son Stephen, who gave up some of their time with me to allow me to write it.

Table of Contents

First Words

I have a confession to make. I've been keeping something to myself that was meant to be shared with others. If I didn't tell you about it, I would be guilty of a terrible sin.

Can you imagine discovering a gold mine in your own back yard? Suppose you were digging a new garden or planting a shrub, and your shovel struck gold—lots of it. No doubt you would be overjoyed as you envisioned paying off your car and house. Within minutes you'd probably be imagining yourself living in a *bigger* house and driving a *nicer* car.

But what if you discovered more gold than you could possibly ever want or need? I'm talking about *tons* of gold. Now remember, you didn't earn it. You didn't deserve it. You were just planting tomatoes.

If you discovered *tons* of gold in your backyard, you'd probably start thinking about your relatives. You'd contemplate paying off their debts and sending them on vacations to Hawaii. Think of how your mother-in-law would approve.

And if there were enough gold, you'd probably start wondering how you could help your friends and neighbors. Maybe you could put some of their children through college.

Or wouldn't it be fun to buy everyone on the block a brand new Cadillac?

A few years ago I discovered a wonderful secret, and it changed everything for me. I mean *everything*. I know other people who know about the secret, and it has revolutionized their lives as well.

This secret was meant to be shared. There is no justification for keeping quiet about it—which is why I've written this book.

I suspect that there are others like myself—those who know the secret but have kept it to themselves. They feel guilty, just like me.

One of those people may love you very much—so much that he or she has given you this book, hoping you would come to share in the knowledge that has changed his or her life.

Like me, your friend, neighbor, or loved one is saying to you: *Please forgive me for waiting so long to tell you this.*

David S. Kirkwood

ONE

There is No God
and Other Tall Tales

I am wearing a very unusual wristwatch as I type these words. Although it looks like an ordinary Seiko, it didn't originate from a factory in Japan as do other Seiko watches.

My watch wasn't designed by anyone, nor did anyone have anything to do with its assembly. My Seiko watch *just happened.*

Let me tell you about it.

A few summers ago, I was walking barefoot along a beach in northern Oregon. The weather was perfect. The view was breath-taking. I can still picture the rugged grandeur of the coastline and the massive cliffs standing against the tide of the surging ocean.

Finding a comfortable spot, I sat down on the warm sand and leaned against the base of a high cliff. As I rested there enjoying the sunshine, suddenly a small rock broke loose from the edge of the cliff and began tumbling down toward me. (I later realized that little rock must have been high in iron and tin content.)

What happened next was amazing to witness. That little rock tumbled at a perfect velocity and bounced at such precise angles that little cogs, springs, hammers, a stem and a watch casing broke off from it—all perfectly formed! You can imagine my surprise.

Even more amazing was the fact that the wind was blowing in such an unusual manner that all those perfectly formed pieces landed together on the beach beside me. I watched in wonder as they fell on top of one another in such a way that a wristwatch was assembled and immediately began ticking! Not only that—the hands of the watch had *just happened* to fall in place at the correct time! I could scarcely believe my eyes.

One chunk had apparently broken off from the rock during its tumble and had amazingly struck a piece of flint near a bird's nest in a crag. As a result, a spark had ignited the straw-filled nest! The heat from the fire had fused the zinc and copper portion of that small rock and formed liquid brass, which began dripping from its height to the beach below. As it did, some drops of liquified brass *just happened* to drop on the casing of that newly-formed watch, coating it perfectly.

As I stared at the gleaming timepiece lying in the sand beside me, I suddenly felt a tremor like a small earthquake. Soon a small crack formed behind me at the base of the cliff.

I watched in astonishment as molten magma poured out of the crack and trickled in a small stream down the beach to the water. Due to the magma's intense heat some of the silicon particles in the sand melted, forming a small piece of transparent glass. I marveled when I realized it would fit perfectly over the face of the wristwatch.

Before I could reach for the small, round piece of glass, a wave from the in-coming tide washed ashore and picked it up. To my surprise the surf gently tumbled the crystal onto the

14

watch, where it snapped perfectly in place!

I was ecstatic to see all these coincidences happening before my eyes. But there is still more to tell.

Strangely enough, a cow, which must have somehow escaped from its pasture, came wandering up the beach. To my utter shock, when it stood before me, the cow suddenly suffered a heart-attack and died. As the animal fell in its final death throes, it landed on two sharp pieces of rock jutting out of the sand.

I watched in astonishment as two thin pieces of leather were simultaneously ripped from the cow's hide. Not only that, both leather strips fell off in such a way that they attached themselves to the newly-formed watch on either side, forming a perfect-looking watch band!

I know this all seems difficult to believe, but I saw it happen with my own eyes.

Finally, I witnessed six red ants march out from a nearby rock and dutifully eat six little holes, all in a row, through one of those leather bands. These, of course, made precise openings for the brass clasp. (I forgot to mention that the clasp had also formed from the brass drippings and had fallen in such a way that it was perfectly attached to the other leather band!)

So now you know the origins of my wristwatch.

Do you believe my story? Of course you don't, and neither do I. The truth is, my Seiko watch was manufactured. Although I've *never seen* any of the Japanese men and women who designed and assembled it, I'm quite sure they exist.

I'm convinced there were intelligent watch designers and assemblers because I can see an intelligent design and assembly in the final product! To believe that somehow my wristwatch "just happened" is irrational and requires a leap of faith that transcends all sound logic. If I sincerely believed my watch just happened, you'd be forced to question my intelligence.

You probably realize what I'm leading up to: *We know that God exists because He is plainly revealed in His amazing creation.* Anyone who is honest with himself will have to admit there is a Creator.

Who Believes in God?

Isaac Newton was undoubtedly one of the most intelligent men of his day and is still revered by the learned. It is reported that he once constructed a small model of our solar system, using globes that all revolved around one central sphere. By means of rods, cogwheels, and belts, all the model planets simultaneously orbited the model sun in this ingenious contraption. Even the orbits of the planets were to some degree proportionate to the orbits of the actual planets in our solar system.

An agnostic friend, upon seeing the contraption remarked, "Newton, what an amazing little invention! Who made it for you?"

Newton replied, "Nobody!"

"What do you mean, 'Nobody'?"

"I mean, nobody made it for me! It just happened! All these cogs and belts and rods and spheres just came together, and by coincidence, they all began revolving in their set orbits just like the planets they represent!"

His unbelieving friend got the message.

According to a recent Gallup Poll, ninety-four percent of all Americans believe there is a God. Six percent say they don't believe or are unsure. If you put those six percent on an airplane that is about to crash-land, the majority will become believers in God before the plane hits the ground. And all the remaining ones will become believers within moments *after their death.* In fact, every single atheist or agnostic who has died is now a believer in God.

Please, if you are one of those six percent who is still alive, give me a chance to persuade you of God's existence before you have no choice but to believe it!

If you already believe in God, let me take you on a tour of some of the wonders of His universe.

Apple Trees and Honeybees

Have you ever bit into a crisp autumn apple and thought about the fact that a good portion of what you are eating is made from the *dirt* of the ground? It's true. Apples, as well as all other fruits and vegetables, are primarily formed from substances within the soil.

How do those substances travel through the roots, trunk, and branches of the apple tree, against gravity? And how does the apple tree know to form apples, rather than oranges or watermelons? Why doesn't it occasionally make a lemon by mistake?

Not only does the apple tree build apples from dirt, but the apple tree itself is primarily formed from the soil—the wood, the bark, the leaves, and even the soft white petals of the apple blossoms. How is that possible?

Even more remarkable is the fact that the fragrance of the blossoms is soil that has experienced an aromatic metamorphosis! When you think about what God is doing every day with soil, the story of Adam being formed from the dust of the ground isn't so hard to swallow.

You probably know the apple tree can't produce its crop without some outside help. *Someone* determined that the lowly honeybee, seeking nectar for its comb, would unwittingly pollinate the apple blossoms.

The little bee himself is quite remarkable. Once he discovers a tree full of blossoms, he travels back to his hive and performs a mysterious dance. That bee ballet enlightens a buzzing audience, and off they fly, knowing the proper direction and exact distance of the waiting nectar.

How does the apple tree know *when* to blossom? Who

programmed it to monitor the temperature and period of the daylight so that it doesn't blossom in the winter or fall?

Possibly the most astonishing fact about the apple tree is this: Protected within each fruit there are little data-banks of information—we call them seeds—that contain all the secrets needed to grow another apple tree. Who among men has been able to unlock the secrets of a single apple seed?

Of course, the apple tree is not the Creator's only witness. There is an infinite variety of mysteries under the sun, and each one calls our attention to an amazing God. He's left His signature on everything He's designed.

"Coincidences" of Nature

How does the salmon, after swimming two thousand miles in the open sea, find the river, then the tributary, and finally the stream of her birth, where, as her ancestors, she will lay her eggs? And what is it that drives her to fight relentless rapids and return to a place she hasn't seen in years only to spawn and quickly die?

The water that forms those rapids hides some secrets of its own. You probably know that sidewalks and bridges contract as they get colder and expand when they get warmer. But why is it that water, unlike practically every other substance, expands just before it freezes? No one knows, but it's a good thing it does, or else ice would be denser than water and wouldn't float.

If ice didn't float, it would sink to the bottom of lakes after crystallizing on the surface. When the spring thaw arrived, some ice on the lake bottoms would remain frozen. As this cycle repeated itself over a period of years, eventually every northern lake, and then every southern lake, would be frozen solid. Earth would enter a permanent and progressively harsher ice-age. As a result, life wouldn't be so pleasant in the Bahamas, or any place else for that matter.

I'm glad God designed the molecular structure of water a

little differently than He did everything else!

There are so many other "coincidences" of nature that volumes could be written detailing them.

Think about our sun for a moment. As big as it looks, it's actually much larger than you can imagine. If it were hollow, it could contain 1,300,000 Earths. Although it is about *ninety-three million miles* away, you can feel its warmth on your face. The light that illuminates our days takes about eight minutes to reach us from the sun, traveling at a speed of 186,000 miles *per second*.

What if the sun were closer? You only have to ask someone who's been to the next-closest planet to the sun, Venus. The surface temperature of Venus averages about 875 degrees. They say that vacationers tan rather quickly there.

What if the sun were further away? On Mars, the next-farthest planet from the sun, the mercury dips to about minus 200. The folks in Minnesota ought to count their blessings.

Speaking of distances, did you know that the moon, too, is obviously positioned very strategically for our sakes? If it were just a little bit closer (relatively speaking), the tides would tend to put a damper on everything. Miami would be under water for twelve hours each day due to the moon's increased gravitational pull on the Atlantic Ocean. And when the tide came in, it would rush like a tidal wave.

Countless other integral phenomena—from the speed of Earth's rotation to the Earth's specific diameter—indicate that Someone carefully calculated what would be needed for life on this planet. Honest, intelligent people just can't stick their heads in the sand and pretend the facts aren't there. In fact, we don't need to look further than our own bodies to see ample evidence of God's handiwork.

The Amazing Human Machine

The human body is made up of a hundred trillion amazingly complex cells. Each cell is comprised of an organized grouping of molecules, which are in themselves highly structured and complex.

Every cell nucleus contains an identical strand of what scientists call DNA, the hereditary set of molecules that instructs every cell in the body as to its function. It is estimated that if the instructions of *each* strand of DNA were written out, they would fill at least one thousand, six-hundred page volumes.

Think about that. Your entire body could be reassembled from the information contained in a single cell!

The DNA strands are less than a trillionth of an inch thick, but if unwound, each cell contains a strand that would stretch about two yards. If all the DNA in your body were attached end to end, it would stretch from the earth to the sun over eight hundred times!

Every cell in your body has a certain specific function. Let's consider the cells in your eyes for a moment. How is it possible that you can read these words? It requires millions of miracles.

Inside your eyeball there are about 107,000,000 cells. About seven million of those cells are called *cones*, which you use to see in daylight. They are color-sensitive, and you can distinguish a thousand different shades of color. The other one hundred million are called *rods*, which you use to see in dim light. They aren't color-sensitive, which is why things tend to look black and white at night.

As light enters the eye, the lens refracts an upside-down image upon the cones and rods. These images are then translated into little electronic messages that travel along some five hundred thousand neurons and nerve paths to take their information to the brain.

The computer inside your head then assembles millions of simultaneous bits of data, merges them with the slightly different data from the other eye, and assembles it into one three-dimensional picture. Then your brain flips the image over so that everything is right-side-up, and somehow sight is accomplished!

The front of the eye always needs to stay moist, so the brain monitors its dryness and sends a signal to activate the eye-lid whenever it's needed. A person might blink three billion times during his life but never needs to think consciously about doing it.

Incidentally, every cell in your body at this moment, except the brain and nerve cells, has been replaced within the last ten years. Quite literally, you're not the person you used to be! You've been replaced! And every cell contains the identical DNA instructions you inherited at conception, when you were comprised of only two cells.

Those two cells divided and duplicated themselves until you were seven pounds of the most complex species God ever created, complete with integrated circulatory, glandular, digestive, nervous, immune, skeletal, lymphatic, respiratory, muscular, and reproductive systems!

The Blind Faith of Atheism

Speaking of conception, I'm always sadly amused when I read some skeptic's objections to the virgin birth of Jesus Christ.

They say, "How is such a birth possible?"

I say, "How is *any* birth possible?"

There must be a million individual miracles connected with the conception, development, and birth of a baby. Why would anyone doubt the virgin birth just because God eliminated one miracle, one time, from the millions of miracles necessary for every baby to be born?

Pulling off the virgin birth was no more difficult for God than any other birth; in fact, it might have been a little easier, requiring one less miracle. Personally, I'd like to meet someone who can simply explain how a five-minute-old baby knows how to nurse.

The atheist actually displays more faith than the most zealous religious fanatic. To believe that there is no God takes infinitely more faith than to believe God exists. Why? Because all the evidence must be ignored. Atheism is the epitome of blind faith.

Why do some people remain steadfast atheists in the light of so much evidence that is contrary to their belief? Simply because they are smart enough to realize that if there is a God, then He shouldn't be ignored. If He created us, then He has a right to tell us how we should live.

Hopefully, since I started this chapter, the already small percentage of atheists has now grown even smaller, and we're ready to go on to the next chapter.

§

"In the absence of any other proof, the thumb alone would convince me of God's existence." *Isaac Newton*

TWO

Open Your Eyes

God exists. So what is He like?

Thankfully, God has not left us in the dark concerning His character, personality, or attributes. The Bible affirms that anyone can figure out something about what God is like by looking at what He has made:

> For since the creation of the world His [God's] invisible attributes, His eternal power and divine nature, have been clearly seen, being understood through what has been made, so that they are without excuse (Romans 1:20).

So what does creation specifically reveal about God, beyond the fact that He exists? First of all, we can easily see that God must be extremely powerful, as the above scripture verse states.

What was your reaction the last time you heard a window-rattling boom of thunder nearby? Your heart probably skipped a few beats. But does thunder scare God? Of course not, since He's the one who invented it.

It stands to reason that the Creator is *superior* to the thing created. So we can certainly conclude that God is more powerful than thunder and lightning.

But let's not stop there.

God must be more powerful than the most powerful thing we can imagine because, whatever we can think of, God created it. If He made something powerful, He must have *greater* power to have created it.

He must be more powerful than the force of a raging hurricane or a twisting tornado. He must be more powerful than the force of the surging tides or the torque of the spinning Earth. He must be more powerful than the gravity of the sun or the combined gravity of every star in every galaxy. He must be more powerful than the nuclear energy that would be released if every atom in the universe was split.

How powerful is God? Words fall short of adequate description. That is why theologians use the term *omnipotent*, meaning "all-powerful."

Within the same line of reasoning, it is evident to everyone that God is great. That, too, is an understatement. Think about the immensity of the universe God has made. Even if you can grasp how great the universe is, you still haven't grasped how great God is. Why? Because He made it all, and, therefore, must be greater.

Star Travel

How immense is the universe? Before we tackle that question, let's consider just our solar system.

It takes light from the sun, traveling at 186,000 miles per second, about five hours to reach the planet farthest out in our solar system, Pluto. If there were an interstate highway from Earth to Pluto, and you drove sixty-five miles an hour the whole way, it would take you over six thousand years to make the trip, one way.

Let's travel a little farther out. The nearest star to us (other than the sun) is Alpha Centauri, and the light shining from it takes over four years to reach us. When you look at Alpha Centauri, you're really seeing it as it looked four years ago. But Alpha Centauri is just a short hop from Earth compared to some other places in our universe.

Our solar system is not too far from the outer edge of the Milky Way galaxy, a group of *billions* of gravitationally bound stars that slowly circle a densely-clustered core. Our little solar system makes the complete swing around the galaxy about once every 230 million years.

How big is our galaxy? At least *one hundred thousand light-years* in diameter. And the Milky Way is just *one* galaxy out of *billions* in the known universe.

Galaxies cluster in groups, of which there are millions, and they in turn cluster in "superclusters." So just how big is the known universe? Nobody knows.

Astronomers have discovered that the universe is constantly increasing in size, indicating that it had a beginning. Presently, it would take at least *twenty billion years* to travel across it—that's if you traveled at the speed of light.

When you look up in the sky at night, you're looking back across the ages of time. Many of the stars in our own galaxy are as much as 80,000 light years away. That means you are actually seeing those stars as they looked 80,000 years ago because that's how long ago their light started its journey to us.

How great is God? He *must* be even greater than His creation. He must be greater than the universe.

A Mad Scientist?

God is also, quite obviously, very intelligent. Once again, that is an understatement, which is why theologians use the word *omniscient*, meaning "all-knowing."

25

Even if you could catalogue the combined knowledge of every person, you still wouldn't know a fraction of what God knows. There is nothing that is a mystery to Him because He's the one who designed and created everything.

God knows the answer to every riddle of science and nature. He's the one who calculated the gravitational pull that one galaxy would exert upon another, and He planned the complicated molecular structure of the DNA in every cell of every living thing. If, as scientists tell us, every cell in your body contains the DNA-coded instructions for the function of the trillions of other cells, then God must be more intelligent than any of us can begin to imagine. Talk about microtechnology!

Furthermore, it stands to reason that such an intelligent Creator, who has blessed His creatures with a limited amount of wisdom, must have an *infinite* degree of wisdom. Since God created us, *He must have an ultimate plan for us.* He must have some objective He is working toward—an ultimate goal.

Surely He couldn't be a mad scientist performing a complicated, colossal experiment. The creation is too complex— too much planning went into small details—even to suggest that we are part of a temporary game or nonsensical whim.

There *must* be a reason God created us.

The Love of God

God must also be loving. How can we deduce His love just from looking at His creation?

First of all, God has been good to you and me. As the apostle Paul once stated in a sermon, "...and yet He [God] did not leave Himself without witness, in that *He did good* and gave you rains from heaven and fruitful seasons, satisfying your hearts with food and gladness" (Acts 14:17; italics mine).

Rain and food are evidences of God's kindness toward us.

Every glad heart is a tribute to love He has shown.

Most of us have taken God's goodness for granted, but we shouldn't. He could have given us only onions to eat, breakfast, lunch, and dinner! And with the wave of His hand, God could shut off global rainfall *permanently*.

The summer before last, the city where I live endured thirty days of drought. When it finally did rain, *everyone* appreciated it. Even a TV weatherman reportedly said "Hallelujah!" right on the air.

My point is, God has been good to you and me, and we should be thankful.

Why is God good? Because God is loving.

Second, we have to suspect that if we, as God's creatures, can know and experience love, then so must He. Surely the most sublime of all human emotions is not foreign to the One who created all humans.

Most people have never thought long about it, but why does a mother love her new-born baby? Is it just a special mixture of chemicals in her brain that causes her to love her child—a love that would cause her to give her own life if need be to save that child? No, her love is instinctive, given to her by God.

If love is the supreme emotion, if love is what the world constantly sings about and dreams of, if love is the binding force of families and friends, then surely the Creator of love is Himself the very personification of love.

The Bible confirms what creation preaches: "God is love" (1 John 4:8).

God is Moral

Finally, we can deduce that if God is love, then He must be moral and upright. Why? Because His perfect love would require that He love everyone equally. If God loved one person more than He loved another, then He wouldn't be perfect in love.

Consequently, perfect love cannot remain passive when

injustice is committed. If one person whom God loves takes selfish advantage of another person whom God loves, then God must react. If He has no reaction, then He can be rightfully accused of endorsing injustice and therefore of being imperfect in love.

Perfect love *must* establish a standard of conduct, a code of ethics, that it expects the objects of its love to obey.

That standard of conduct, which God has established, is universally known: "Do unto others as you would have them do unto you." When we act in our own self-interest to the degree that others are hurt, God—who in perfect love loves everyone equally— declares we have sinned.

That universally-known *law of love* is not something one has to be taught—it is instinctive. We call its voice our *conscience.* All of us are born with this law written on our hearts because it has been given to us by God. That should be obvious to anyone who has ever heard a two year old protest, "That's not fair!" He is voicing the ubiquitous internal belief that injustice is not right and selfishness is wrong.

The God who gave every person a conscience is indeed moral and upright. He wouldn't deposit an instinctive code of ethics within His creatures unless He Himself lived by that same code. Otherwise He'd be hypocritical.

If God isn't moral and upright, then He isn't perfect; He isn't loving; and He isn't God.

The knowledge of all these attributes of God can be obtained without ever reading the Bible, listening to a sermon, or acquiring a degree in philosophy. All we need do is open our God-given eyes, turn on our God-given brain, and listen to our God-given conscience.

§

"The heavens are telling of the glory of God; and their expanse is declaring the work of His hands. Day to day pours forth speech, and night to night reveals knowledge" (Psalm 19:1-2).

THREE

The Sinners Club

B efore the collapse of communism in Eastern Europe, I spent some time traveling in Poland, East Germany, Czechoslovakia, and Romania. I listened to the stories of those who were imprisoned behind miles of barbed wire, machine guns, and land mines—the communist insurance policy that no one could escape their "utopian society" without paying with his life.

Many with whom I spoke were suffering persecution because of their faith. Most people had no choice but to stand for hours in food lines in the bitter cold, and almost all were afraid to speak against those in authority. I witnessed the poverty, the misery, and the hopelessness of people who never seemed to smile and lived where everything was cloudy and gray.

Yet, with disgust, I saw the perks of the privileged party members who lived in this supposed "classless society," and

I thought about the hypocrisy of it all. It seemed to me that the communist leaders who denounced the evils of capitalism were the worst capitalists of all—they exploited their own people for the sake of self-centered gain.

I've also done some traveling in Central America and discovered why some of the people, to my great surprise, are so open to the ideas of communism. Why? Because they are the victims of greedy capitalists, whose profits claimed a higher priority than the welfare of the impoverished people who made their profits possible—people who have no hope of escape from a system they are convinced is evil.

It dawned on me that the real evil isn't inherent in either economic system. Communists supposedly want equality for all, and capitalists, in theory, want everyone to have an equal opportunity. Still, both systems inevitably create people who get rich at the expense of others. Both systems have brought out the worst of man's greed and selfishness.

Capitalist pigs or communist hogs, it makes no difference—they'll both push you into the mud to get their mouths in the slop. It's not the economic theories that are inherently evil—it's the men who use the systems to accomplish their selfish ends, regardless of who suffers in the process.

Better Than the Rest?

The same is true when we examine democracy and dictatorship. History teaches, as Lord Action said, that "Power tends to corrupt and absolute power corrupts absolutely." Oh, how we Americans deplore the human rights violations of third-world dictators!

Democracy, however, doesn't automatically create incorruptible leaders, as we who live in the United States all know. It seems we are constantly barraged with news reports concerning those in our government who have committed some breach of ethics. You can't help but wonder, if you put those same people in a different country under a different political system, would they be erecting barbed wire fences along their borders?

Winston Churchill made the astute observation: "Democracy is the worst system ever invented, except for all the rest." How true. And what is it that makes democracy the worst system, except for all the rest? (Or in other words, what makes it better?)

Democracy provides a system of checks and balances. These add some extra incentives for leaders to walk the straight and narrow path while providing a safeguard for the citizens when its leaders don't. That's why a democracy is superior to a dictatorship—we can oust those rascals before they do too much damage!

Both dictatorships and democracies, like communism and capitalism, unmask an inherent evil in people. Given an opportunity to take advantage of someone else, the average person will normally seize the opportunity—if he's reasonably certain he won't suffer any negative repercussions.

And don't we just love talking about those *dirty* politicians and their *dirty* deeds? We certainly do. But when I call them "dirty politicians," I've unmasked myself.

Stop for a moment and picture this scene: Imagine a thrice-convicted felon behind bars who denounces his fellow-inmates as "lawbreakers." What is your reaction? No doubt you immediately think to yourself, "Why, he has no right to denounce his fellow inmates as lawbreakers because he's just as guilty."

Now let's go back to talking about those *dirty* politicians. Do I really have a right to condemn a politician for using his position for selfish ends? I don't, unless I've never taken selfish advantage of another person or selfishly capitalized on a favorable circumstance. But I have. So when I condemn the dirty politician, *I'm no different than the felon who denounces his fellow inmates as "lawbreakers."* It's just one more case of the pot calling the kettle black.

"You Are the Man!"

Now don't pretend to sit there with a halo over your head. You too, my dear reader, are just as guilty as I am of this universal sin. All of us have acted in our own self-interest at one time or another, and others have suffered because of it. Everyone of us is guilty, either more or less. And to add sin to our sin, we've self-righteously denounced others who've acted just as we have. And that makes us hypocrites.

This is precisely the pandemic sin of which the apostle Paul was speaking in the following verse:

> Therefore you are without excuse, every man of you who passes judgment, *for in that you judge another, you condemn yourself; for you who judge practice the same things* (Romans 2:1; italics mine).

It is essential to grasp this important truth. When we point out the sins of others, we are openly testifying before the court of heaven that we *know* there is such a thing as right and wrong. Our own judgments of others provide incontestable evidence of our belief in a universal code of ethics, a standard of conduct which we ourselves have broken many times. Consequently, our own judgments of others are self-condemning.

Do you remember hearing the story in the Bible of the time King David committed adultery with Uriah's wife, Bathsheba? She got pregnant, so David arranged for her husband's murder on the battlefield. It appeared that Uriah died because of the misfortunes of war, but his death had been pre-arranged by King David, his commander-in-chief, who then lawfully married Uriah's grieving widow.

David's devious plan seemed to go smoothly, until one day God sent a prophet named Nathan to visit him. Nathan asked King David for his judgment concerning a very rich man in his kingdom who had great flocks of sheep but who had taken the single lamb of a poor neighbor in order to set a meal before one of his guests. David was furious and righteously declared the rich man should suffer death for his deed.

The prophet then pointed his finger at David and cried out, *"You are the man!"*

David's story has universal application, because every time you and I condemn someone else, the Sovereign Spirit of Justice points His finger at us and cries out, *"You are the man!"*

As a wise person once rightfully said, "When you point your finger at someone else, take note that three of your own fingers are pointed straight back at you."

The Root of the Problem

Do you feel convicted? You should. If you don't, something is wrong.

Chances are, if you are like most of us, when you feel conviction for sin, you try to justify yourself. Perhaps you're saying, "But I've never committed adultery or murder like David." Maybe you haven't. But there is one sin that is the root of all other sins, and that is *selfishness*. The root cause of David's sins was selfishness; he was "looking out for number one."

How does God feel about selfishness? Jesus said that the second greatest commandment is that we should love our neighbor as ourselves (see Matthew 22:36-40). The Bible says that the commandment to love unselfishly sums up *all* the commandments of the Old Testament:

> ...he who loves his neighbor has fulfilled the law. For this, "You shall not commit adultery, You shall not murder, You shall not steal, You shall not covet," and if there is any other commandment, it is summed up in the saying, "You shall love your neighbor as yourself." Love does no wrong to a neighbor; love therefore is the fulfillment of the law (Romans 13:8-10).

33

People commit adultery and murder, and they steal and covet as a result of their *selfishness*. God hates selfishness because He is unselfish love personified, and, therefore, doesn't love one person more than any other. When an act of selfishness is committed, injustice takes place. And when we commit any act of selfishness, we are guilty of the same sinful motivation as the adulterer or murderer.

Jesus whole-heartedly endorsed this truth in His famous "Sermon on the Mount." His listeners then weren't any different than you or I. Maybe we haven't committed murder. Maybe we haven't committed adultery. But listen to what the Son of God said:

> "You have heard that the ancients [ancestors] were told, 'You shall not commit murder' and 'Whoever commits murder shall be liable to the court.'
>
> "*But I say to you* that everyone who is angry with his brother shall be guilty before the court; and whoever shall say to his brother, 'Empty-head,' shall be guilty before the supreme court; and whoever shall say, 'You fool,' *shall be guilty enough to go into the hell of fire"* (Matthew 5:21-22; italics mine).

I didn't say that—Jesus did. And according to Him, a person isn't guiltless just because he's never committed murder. The same hate that condemns the murderer to hell also condemns the angry man. Both are selfish. Jesus didn't stop there:

> "You have heard that it was said, 'You shall not commit adultery'; but I say to you, that every one who *looks* on a woman to lust for her has committed adultery with her already *in his heart"* (Matthew 5:27-28; italics mine).

The same selfishness that commits adultery is the same selfishness that lusts.

34

Throwing the First Stone

Perhaps you know the New Testament story of the woman caught in adultery. The Pharisees had caught her in the very act, and then brought her before Jesus in order to trap Him. They reminded Jesus that the law of Moses commanded such a woman be stoned to death.

Jesus' profound reply was simply the restatement of a principle that all of us know to be true: *No one has a right to condemn another when he himself is guilty.* Jesus said it like this: "He who is without sin among you, let him be the first to throw a stone at her" (John 8:7).

After He spoke, Jesus knelt down and wrote in the dust. The Bible says that the woman's accusers slowly began to depart, first the oldest ones and then the younger ones. What was it that Jesus wrote in the dust? I wonder, could it have been the names of the women in the Pharisees' fantasies? Was it the names of their girlfriends?

Regardless, two things become evident in this incident.

First of all, adultery is sin. Once everyone was gone, Jesus told the woman, "Go and *sin no more.*"

Second, to condemn others is a sin. The self-righteous men who were holding the stones that day deserved to be stoned every bit as much as the woman they were about to execute. That is how it always is.

All of us are guilty of passing judgment upon others for doing what we have likewise done: acted in our own self-interest. All of us are like the off-duty policeman who speeds home after issuing speeding tickets all day to irate motorists.

Like it or not, we're all members of the sinners club. And some who think they don't belong are actually the highest-ranking officers—which is why Jesus so frequently denounced self-righteous people. (Incidentally, He is the *only* one who had the right to denounce hypocrites—because He was sinless.)

35

God's Point of View

You may be asking yourself, "Why is this author trying to make me feel so guilty?" The answer is this: You must see the truth about *your own sin* in order to understand fully your need for a Savior.

I'm not going to leave you eternally guilty. In fact after two more chapters I'm going to tell you the best news that has ever been heard by a human ear. I'm leading up to God's plan to offer you a free pardon—full forgiveness—and an eternally guaranteed place in heaven. But of absolute necessity, you must see yourself a sinner who needs God's pardon.

Some people are like the cowering adulteress—she knew she was guilty and was bracing herself to feel the first stone bruise her back. But most others are like the crowd that had gathered to condemn the woman, equally deserving of the punishment they hypocritically wanted to execute upon her.

Just as the apostle Paul said, they were self-condemned and without excuse.

Now picture the scene as God saw it: There stood a group of lustful men and adulterers preparing to stone an adulteress! What pure hypocrisy! But isn't that a picture of the human race?

Gossipers gossip about their gossipy neighbors. Lazy workers (who steal time from their boss) complain about the extravagant salary of their CEO. Holier-than-thou types don't go to church because "everyone there thinks he is holier-than-thou." Lustful editors write about fallen evangelists. Citizens cheat on their taxes so as not to give more money to "the corrupt government." Electors complain about the self-seeking politicians whom they elected to serve their own self-interests.

I recently read in the crime report of a local newspaper about three people who reported the theft of their radar detectors from their cars. They were angry because someone broke the law, stealing from them a device that helped them break the law!

All of us have acted selfishly, all of us have condemned and criticized others, and thus all of us are self-condemned before God. It's not just the communists; it's not just the greedy capitalists; and it's not just the dirty politicians.

We're all guilt-carrying members of the sinners club. Membership has its consequences.

§

"...for all have sinned and fall short of the glory of God" (Romans 3:23).

FOUR

The Angel
on Your Shoulder

"Who says it's wrong to have sex with someone else's wife? I can do my own thing. There are no such things as moral absolutes. I'm not bound by the rules invented by some ancient religious kill-joys."

If I could find someone who really believed that philosophy to the degree that he lived it out *consistently*, then I'd listen to him. But I haven't found a person yet, who in his every day life, consistently walks and talks as if there really are no moral absolutes.

The most hedonistic playboy still has a code of ethics that he limitedly lives by and that he expects others to live by. As I have said previously, that code of ethics is built in by God. Whether we want to admit it or not, *we all know exactly what is right and what is wrong.*

Let's take the playboy who says he sees nothing wrong with having an affair with another man's wife. His motto is,

39

"If it feels good, do it." If he *really* believes there are no moral absolutes, then he should never complain when other people who've adopted the same motto commit selfish acts that hurt *him*. If I decide to take a sledgehammer and smash the windshield of his car, then he has no right to criticize me. If he does, I'll just say, "Hey, I felt like doing it. It made me feel good. And besides, there are no such things as moral absolutes. There is no right and wrong. I'm not going to be bound by some stupid law that some ancient kill-joy invented."

How do you think that playboy would react to *my* line of reasoning? He'd object violently because he believes in a code of ethics. It's not right to destroy another man's property. Everyone in the world knows that, even people who live in the most primitive societies. Furthermore, people have *always* known that it is wrong to act in their own self-interest if others are harmed in the process.

What Makes a Wrong, Wrong?

Our founding fathers expressed it eloquently when they penned, "We hold these truths to be self-evident, that all men are created equal..." These truths *are* self-evident. Selfishness is wrong because all men, created in God's image, are equal—equally loved by God.

When we act on our own behalf in such a way that causes others to suffer, we have sinned. That is what makes stealing wrong. That is what makes lying wrong. That is what makes adultery wrong. That is what makes gossiping wrong. That is what makes abortion wrong. Practically every law that has ever existed has been based upon the underlying principle that there are self-evident moral absolutes—particularly that selfish acts that harm others are morally wrong.

When the hedonistic playboy stands before God, the Creator won't buy his excuse that he didn't know what was right and what was wrong. God will have volumes of incontrovertible evidence from the man's daily life proving his obvious belief in a standard of conduct. Every time the man criticized another person for acting selfishly, his own words testified of his belief in moral absolutes and thus condemned him.

That is precisely what will take place at his judgment before God. God has a record of each man's every careless word.

Read what Jesus said:

"And I say to you, that every *careless* word that men shall speak, they shall render account for it in the day of judgment. For by your words you will be justified, *and by your words you will be condemned*" (Matthew 12:36-37; italics mine).

Now before we self-righteously condemn every self-seeking playboy, don't forget that all of us are in the same boat, either stern or aft. All of us have broken the sacred rule that Jesus said sums up the moral teaching of the Old Testament: "Do unto others as you want them to do unto you." In the last chapter we learned that all of us stand self-condemned before God because of our own judgments of others.

Who Decided?

Let's answer the question of where the idea of moral absolutes originated. Who decided that selfishness is wrong?

Let's look specifically at adultery. Was it some ancient religious kill-joy who decided that adultery is a sin? If it was, then which one was it?

Was it the prudish New England Puritans who dreamed it up? No.

Was it a group of ascetic monks in the dark ages? No.

Did Jesus introduce it? No.

Surely it must have begun with Moses and the Ten

Commandments. No, it didn't.

You see, archaeologists have uncovered the civil codes of several ancient cultures, codes that even predate the Ten Commandments by *hundreds* of years. Probably the most well-known example would be the Code of Hammurapi (an ancient king of Babylon).

Discovered in 1901 by French archaeologist Jacques de Morgan, the Code contained 282 laws inscribed upon a stone shaft, dated around 1750 B.C., and now preserved in the Louvre in Paris.

And what did Hammurapi, who lived three to five centuries before the Ten Commandments were given, have to say on the subject of adultery? Read it for yourself:

> If the wife of a man has been caught while lying with another man, they shall bind them [together] and throw them into the water.[1]

It's as obvious as a whale in a wading pool: everyone, everywhere, has always known that there are moral absolutes.

So when did the idea originate that selfishness is wrong? As I said in the second chapter, the answer ought to be obvious to anyone who has ever heard a two-year old protest, "That's not fair!"

Every person is born with the knowledge of moral absolutes. That knowledge has been given to him by God, and that is exactly what the Bible teaches.

Written on Your Heart

In the book of Romans, chapter two, the apostle Paul compares God's revelation to the Jews with His revelation to the Gentiles. The Jews were given the Ten Commandments—engraved upon tablets of stone by the finger of God—but the non-Jewish peoples, the Gentiles, never had that privilege. Paul states, however, that every Gentile has had God's law written upon his heart by God Himself. That inward law of God is what we refer to as our *conscience.*

> For when Gentiles who do not have the Law *do instinctively* the things of the Law, these, not having the Law, are a law to themselves, in that they show the work of the Law *written in their hearts,* their *conscience* bearing witness, and their thoughts alternately accusing or else defending them, on the day when, according to my gospel, God will judge the secrets of men through Jesus Christ (Romans 2:14-16, italics mine).

You've no doubt seen the cartoons of the man who has the devil sitting on one shoulder and an angel on the other shoulder, both speaking into opposite ears. Actually there is more theological truth to that picture than many people realize. The error in it is that our moral instructions don't come from the outside—they come from the inside. They are, as Paul said, *instinctive.*

We've all perceived that inward guidance that leads us to resist the temptation to be selfish. Probably everyone has obeyed that inward leading to some degree. But *all of us,* more or less, have violated it more than we care to admit.

Why did God give us a conscience? The apostle Paul revealed the reason in the above-quoted verse, and it only makes logical sense: Someday, God is going to judge men on the basis of whether or not they obeyed their conscience, whether or not they did what they knew they were supposed to do.

Why is that so important to God? Because God has an ultimate plan for a future perfect society, and selfish people won't fit in there. Why? Because God is love. In the final chapter, we'll examine what the Bible has to say concerning this future society.

Of course, since all of us have violated our conscience, we all stand condemned before God, deserving whatever punishment He deems appropriate. There isn't a person reading this book who hasn't acted selfishly. Most of us have led lives that are characterized by selfishness. Even our "good deeds" are often selfishly motivated.

We wine and dine others to get something from them.

We volunteer so we can add a self-promoting paragraph to our resume´.

We obey the law motivated by a fear of getting caught and suffering the consequences—rather than because of true concern for those who would be hurt by our breaking the law.

We give gifts so the recipients will think more highly of us. Too often, our gifts are really bribes. And if we aren't immediately thanked in proportion to the amount spent on the gift, we criticize the recipient behind his back! (Now isn't that unselfish love!)

§

"But realize this, that in the last days difficult times will come. For *men will be lovers of self...*" (II Timothy 3:1-2a; italics mine).

Endnote

1. Samuel Noah Kramer, *Cradle of Civilization*. Alexandria, VA: Time-Life Books, 1978, p. 82.

FIVE

Built Into the System

I'm so glad you've read this far, because your life is about to be radically changed. In fact, your eternal destiny is going to be set on a different course.

Let's sum up what we've learned to this point.

First of all, God exists. That is obvious from looking at all He has created.

Second, God is powerful, great, intelligent, wise, loving, and moral. That, too, is obvious from looking at creation.

Third, all of us know that selfishness is wrong because we are all born with a God-given conscience.

Fourth, all of us stand self-condemned before God because of our own judgments of others. We've criticized them for doing that of which we are just as guilty.

Finally, God is the personification of perfect love, and He *must* react when selfish acts are committed because He loves everyone equally. If He remained passive after witnessing injustice, then He could rightly be accused of loving the offender more than the offended. God, therefore, *must* punish those who act selfishly.

A lot of people have the idea that a loving God would never punish anyone, but you must see that just the opposite is true: A loving God *must* punish selfish acts.

Let's imagine that you are the parent of two children. One of your children is very good, and one is very bad. The bad one is always hurting the good one. In fact, the good one has bruises and open wounds all over his body.

You love both your children, but does that mean you would never punish the bad child for striking the good one? Of course not! If you don't discipline the bad child, the neighbors will say, "The guy next door is a terrible parent. He must not love his child at all." Isn't that right? They'd accuse you of *not* being a loving parent! If you love the child that is being picked on, you'll discipline the selfish one. (And you'll punish the bad child because you love him, too, and don't want him to grow up to be a bully.)

God is no different, except that His love for us far transcends the love that any parent feels for his or her child. *How much more,* therefore, must God punish those who act selfishly! If you believe that God is loving, then you have no choice but to believe also that He will punish those who don't obey Him. If He doesn't punish the disobedient, He isn't loving at all.

Payday's Coming

God's wrath upon evil is another one of those "self-evident truths." He's created a system that delivers automatic wrath upon those who act solely in their own self-interest, regardless of how others suffer. Everybody knows that.

Most drama that has ever been produced for television, the movie theater, or the stage, communicates a fundamental theme of good versus evil. Everybody hopes that the good guys will win and the bad guys will "get what they deserve," which they usually do.

In real life, not every conflict is resolved in one hour, nor are evil acts brought to immediate justice, but payday does come. Those who live by the sword die by the sword. What you sow, you reap. What goes around, comes around.

It's built into the system—selfish people suffer for their selfishness. Sure, some people seemingly "beat the system." They continue on their self-centered path for years. But ultimately, they fall prey to their own devices.

Take the adulterer once more. He has cheated on his wife. He's acted selfishly. What does he suffer? First of all, he automatically suffers a guilty conscience. That conscience was given to him by God. His conscience is part of the built-in system that makes God's punishment of selfishness self-evident.

Can you see it? People don't say, "I'm enjoying life so much because of my guilty conscience." No, they say, "I'm *suffering* with a guilty conscience." Let me say once more that suffering is an indication of the built-in system God has designed to punish selfishness.

The selfish man who has cheated on his wife may also destroy his marriage and lose his children. Not only that, it may cost him financially over the years as he pays alimony and child support. He will suffer the loss of respect from his peers and other family members as well. Can you see that those consequences are all part of the built-in system?

People Pay the Price

Think about this: God didn't have to create us as He did—in His image. We could have been created to procreate without marriage like the moose—with the strongest bull winning the sole privilege to mate with all the females. I know that sounds absurd, but not to a moose! That's the only way he knows to relate when mating time comes around. He doesn't worry about what will happen if he mates with ten

47

females in one season. And why not? Because he isn't created in God's image.

All moose aren't created equal. Survival of the fittest rules their domain. When a bull moose mates with a female that another moose mated with last year, he doesn't have to fear what the adulterous human must fear. The reason? *Because that is how God designed it.* Do you see it? Punishment is built into the human society but not the moose society.

The adulterer also runs the risk of contracting syphilis, gonorrhea, or AIDS. Do you think the bull moose with multipartners worries about those terrible things? Of course not. Why? Because that is how God has designed it.

People who say they don't believe a loving God would punish sin need to open their eyes to reality. Sin is being punished every day. It's built right into the system. Even medical science now tells us that the selfish emotions—such as hatred, bitterness, and jealousy—make our bodies more susceptible to disease. This is more evidence of the fact that God is judging and will judge all sin.

The Bible, in even stronger terms than I've used, asserts this self-evident truth. Read it for yourself:

> For the wrath of God *is* revealed... (Romans 1:18a; italics mine).

Notice it said *"is* revealed," not *"is going to be* revealed." Yes, God's wrath is *going* to be revealed, but the apostle Paul's point in this passage is that God's wrath is being revealed *right now.* Let's keep reading:

> For the wrath of God *is* revealed from heaven against all ungodliness and unrighteousness of men, who suppress the truth in unrighteousness, because that which is known about God is evident within them; for God made it evident to them....but they became futile in their speculations, and their foolish heart was darkened...
>
> ...For this reason God gave them over to *degrading*

passions; for their women exchanged the natural function of that which is unnatural, and in the same way also the men abandoned the natural function of the woman and burned in their desire towards one another, *men with men committing indecent acts and receiving in their own persons the due penalty of their error* (Romans 1:18-19, 21b, 26-27; italics mine).

You don't need to read the Bible to know that homosexuality is wrong. All you need is a basic understanding of human anatomy, and you can easily figure out that males aren't meant to have sex with other males. *That is self-evident.*

Still, men and women in their rebellion toward God will disobey His self-evident laws and ultimately suffer the built-in consequences of their actions. This ought to be especially obvious to our modern world that has been plagued by the AIDS epidemic.

Don't get me wrong, I'm not self-righteously condemning homosexuals because I, too, have rebelled against God's self-evident laws. I, just like you, have disobeyed my conscience, committing many acts of selfishness. And like you, I've suffered the built-in consequences for my sin.

What's That Got to do With Me?

It is obvious for several reasons that God is holy and that He punishes selfishness. What are those reasons?

First, because He *must* punish selfishness if He is a God of love, which He is.

Second, because we can see God's built-in system of punishment—it's part of the structure of our reality.

And *third*, because the Bible confirms what our reality teaches us: God is just and holy, and He *does* and *will* punish all sin. In fact, the Bible has more references to God's anger, fury, and wrath than statements about His love.

What does that mean for you and me? It means that if we

49

have committed any act of selfishness, we must be punished. To what degree must we be punished? Are the built-in punishments that are part of our everyday reality sufficient recompense for our selfish acts?

First of all, we must take into consideration *whom* we have offended. We have offended the Creator of all things, the One who is before all time, the all-powerful and all knowing God.

Second, we must take into consideration the terrible nature of *our sin*. Few of us fully understand how hideous selfishness really is. In God's eyes it is the ugliest, most vile thing there is. It proudly seeks its own well-being, vainly climbing higher while it uses people who are created in God's image as stepping-stones. It is opposed to God's very nature because, as the Bible states, He is unselfish love (1 John 4:8).

Third, we must consider *how much* God loves the ones against whom we've acted selfishly. More than we can understand, God loves those people whom we've used or neglected or judged or hurt. If God let us off easy, then we could conclude He must not really love the people who have suffered because of us.

Fourth, we must take into consideration that God is the epitome of perfect morality and perfect justice. The moral Judge of the universe *must* deliver the full recompense of His broken law.

What does the Bible say concerning we who have passed judgment upon others while at the same time leading lives characterized by selfish ambition? Again, please read for yourself:

> Therefore you are without excuse, every man of you who passes judgment, for in that you judge another, you condemn yourself; for you who judge practice the same things. And we know that *the judgment of God rightly falls upon those who practice such things.* And do you suppose this, O man, when you pass judgment upon those who practice such things and do the same yourself,

50

that *you will escape the judgment of God?* [Now the apostle is writing about God's future judgment.] Or do you think lightly of the riches of His kindness and forbearance and patience, not knowing that the kindness of God leads you to repentance?

But because of your stubbornness and unrepentant heart *you are storing up wrath for yourself in the day of wrath* and revelation of God, who will render to every man according to his deeds: to those who by perseverance in doing good seek for glory and honor and immortality, eternal life; but to those who are *selfishly ambitious* and do not obey the truth, wrath and indignation. There will be *tribulation and distress* for every soul of man who does evil... (Romans 2:1-9; italics mine).

When the apostle Paul writes about future tribulation and distress, it's obvious he means what the Bible calls *hell*.

Going to Hell?

It seems that fewer preachers are mentioning hell any more, but Jesus can never be classed with them. Because He loved His listeners and didn't want them to spend eternity there, Jesus warned them of hell quite frequently.

In the gospel of Matthew alone, I've counted thirty-eight direct or indirect references to God's future judgment and hell.[1] Let me share a few with you. In Matthew 18:8-9, Jesus said:

"And if your hand or your foot causes you to stumble, cut it off and throw it from you; it is better for you to enter life crippled or lame, than having two hands or two feet, to be cast into the *eternal fire*. And if your eye causes you to stumble, pluck it out, and throw it from you. It is better for you to enter life with one eye, than having two eyes, to be cast into *the hell of fire*" (italics mine).

Is it really Jesus' intention that we cut off our hands and pluck out our eyes if they've caused us to sin? If everyone took this command literally, we'd all be blind, lame, and crippled! No, Jesus was using a figure of speech we call *hyperbole*, that is, exaggeration for effect.

When you tell your child, "I must have called you a thousand times before you finally answered me!" that is a hyperbole. You use hyperbole when you want to make a strong point.

Jesus had a particularly strong point that He was trying to make, and that is, "Hell is such a terrible place, it would be worth cutting off your hands and feet and plucking out your eyes to stay out of it." That tells me *hell must be a very horrible place.*

Notice that twice in the above-quoted verses, Jesus described hell as a place of fire. One time He referred to it as an *eternal* fire. In the Greek language, in which the New Testament was originally written, the word translated *hell* is the word "gehenna." All of Jesus' listeners knew exactly what He was talking about when He used that word.

Gehenna was the name for the gigantic heap of garbage in the valley of Hinnom that was just outside the gates of Jerusalem. The constant dumping of Jerusalem's garbage there fed perpetually burning fires. As you can imagine, the rotting refuse and rancid smoke were nauseating, and what the flames didn't consume, maggots and worms fed upon. According to Mark's gospel account, Jesus went on to mention those worms:

> "And if your hand causes you to stumble, cut it off; it is better for you to enter life crippled, than having two hands, to go into hell, *into the unquenchable fire, where their worm does not die, and the fire is not quenched"* (Mark 9:43-44; italics mine).

Jesus loves us, which is why He is so strongly warning us

of the ultimate recompense for our sin. *Hell is a place of eternal, unquenchable fire.* The people who end up there will be punished eternally, just as Jesus also said:

> "Then He will also say to those on His left, 'Depart from Me, accursed ones, into the *eternal fire* which has been prepared for the devil and his angels'....And these will go away into *eternal punishment,* but the righteous into eternal life" (Matthew 25:41, 46; italics mine).

On another occasion, Jesus described further miseries that the unsaved will perpetually suffer:

> "So it will be at the end of the age; the angels shall come forth, and take out the wicked from among the righteous, and will cast them into the furnace of fire; *there shall be weeping and gnashing of teeth*" (Matthew 13:49-50; italics mine).

Some may object, saying, "I don't believe God would punish anyone eternally!"

Those who make such a statement don't understand *Who* it is they have offended—the God of the universe.

Neither do they fully comprehend the terrible nature of their life-long selfishness.

Neither do they realize how much God loves the people against whom they've committed selfish acts.

Neither do they understand God's perfect morality or justice.

Neither do they take into account the incredible mercy that God has shown them all their lives as He has patiently waited for them to repent of their selfish ways.

Neither do they consider how God has repeatedly warned them of their terrible fate through the built-in punishments they have experienced for their selfish acts—namely, a tormenting conscience and all the negative repercussions that result from sin.

Hell on Earth

The temporal suffering that we undergo only serves to warn us of the eternal suffering we will undergo if we continue our selfish lifestyle.

People who say, "I think that this life is all the hell there is," are at least partially correct. The same God who built temporal punishments into the structure of our reality is the same God who will cast the unrighteous into hell. When we suffer for our sins on earth, we are experiencing a little bit of what hell is all about.

Finally, it really doesn't make any difference what anyone thinks. All that matters is *what God has said*. If God says there is an eternal hell where people will suffer eternally, then that's how it is. It makes no difference what anybody thinks, and no one has any right to judge God.

As God Himself said through the prophet Isaiah:

> "Woe to the one who quarrels with his Maker—an earthenware vessel among the vessels of earth! Will the clay say to the potter, 'What are you doing?'" (Isaiah 45:9).

Most importantly, the person who says he thinks that God would never send anyone to an eternal hell has failed to take something else into account: that God has provided a way whereby every person can escape his rightful sentence to hell.

In fact, the price for the provision of that potential escape has been paid by God Himself—who endured the suffering that we deserved in order that mercy might be shown to us.

That is what the next chapter is all about. That is the chapter for which I've been preparing you. Hopefully by now, you are more than ready to respond to God's free offer of forgiveness !

§

54

"For God has shut up all in disobedience that He might show mercy to all. Oh, the depth of the riches both of the wisdom and knowledge of God!" (Romans 11:32-33).

Endnote

1. See Matthew 3:7, 3:10-12, 5:20, 5:22, 5:29, 7:1-2, 7:13-14, 7:19, 7:21-23, 7:26-27, 8:12, 10:15, 10:28, 10:33, 11:22, 11:24, 12:32, 12:36-37, 12:41-42, 13:30, 13:41-42, 13:49-50, 15:13-14, 18:6-9, 18:34-35, 21:41-44, 22:7, 22:11-13, 23:13-15, 23:33, 24:21-31, 24:37-42, 24:48-51, 25:11-13, 25:30, 25:41, 25:46, 26:24

SIX

Born to Die

You've probably seen the movie, *The Ten Command-ments*—if not two or three times, surely you've seen it at least once.

Even if the plot escapes you, more than likely you're familiar with the story of Moses and the exodus of the Israelites from Egyptian slavery. Remember the various plagues—frogs, locusts, hailstones, and so on—that came upon Egypt? Through ten terrible disasters God eventually convinced Pharaoh it was in his best interest to release all his Israelite slaves.

Remember how God split the Red Sea and how Israel passed through on dry ground? Possibly you saw that powerful scene portrayed in Cinemascope or learned about the exodus as a child in Sunday School.

In spite of my exposure to this awesome account of God's power, I remained ignorant of what I now realize is by far the most important aspect of the story of Israel's exodus. The entire drama reveals God's plan for mankind. Furthermore, it portrays aspects of God's character that we have already considered.

Egypt Had it Coming

The book of Exodus begins with the report of Pharaoh's savage plan to reduce Israel's growing population through infanticide. Fearing that Israel would become mightier than Egypt, Pharaoh decreed that every new-born Israeli baby boy was to be cast alive into the Nile River.

Into such tragic times, Moses was born. You may remember how his mother's floating basket made it possible for him to be rescued by Pharaoh's daughter.

About eighty years later, God captured Moses' attention through a burning bush and called him to the task of leading the Israelites from Egypt to the promised land. There was only one problem: Pharaoh didn't want to free his cheap foreign labor force.

Consequently God sent increasingly severe plagues upon Egypt, culminating in the midnight death of all the first-born sons of every Egyptian. Finally, that night Pharaoh and the Egyptians decided to allow the people of Israel to depart from their country.

Some people, who have never thought about it much, have questioned the fairness of God's judgment upon the Egyptians. They ask, "What was so special about the Israelites that God favored them above the Egyptians?"

But the answer is quite obvious: God was acting in perfect love, and, therefore, perfect justice. The Egyptians had selfishly mistreated the Israelites for decades, using people who were created in God's image as their slaves. They had also enforced a barbarous system of infanticide that must have brought untold suffering to the families of Israel. The loving God could not remain passive.

What did the ancient Egyptians deserve? They deserved to

die. People who kill other people's babies deserve to die. Still, God showed them mercy for years, giving them time to repent. Finally He had to act. *Love and justice demanded it.*

God sent Moses to demand Israel's release. When Pharaoh refused, and, in fact, actually increased Israel's labors, God sent the first plague—the waters of Egypt turned into blood. Incredibly, Pharaoh hardened his heart, and God sent a second, and then a third, and then a fourth increasingly severe plague.

After each plague was lifted, Pharaoh repeatedly hardened his heart, and finally the last judgment arrived: all the first-born sons of Egypt died in one night.

Settling the Score

Too many people only see God's judgments in this story. But can you see the incredible mercy of God? Pharaoh could have averted God's final judgment if he had heeded the warning of God's initial, more minor judgments. But he didn't.

I think we'd all agree that Pharaoh and the people of Egypt deserved even worse punishment than they received. In fact, there isn't any doubt that if the death of their first-born sons hadn't convinced them to release the Israelite slaves, then God would have sent a more severe judgment. Ultimately, they would have received what they really deserved: complete annihilation.

Was it fair that all the first-born sons of Egypt died? Yes, the Egyptians were only reaping what they'd sown. Still, they got far less than they deserved.

Every score that is not settled in this life is settled in the next one. The partial settling of the scores in this life serves to warn us that God is *perfectly* fair, and every score will be ultimately settled in the next life.

As the Bible states, God "will render to every man according to his deeds" (Romans 2:6). Of that you can be certain.

No one, and I mean no one, has a right to complain that God has treated him unfairly. Not only has God *not* treated us *unfairly,* but He *has* treated us *very mercifully.*

It's not that we *have* received what we *haven't* deserved, but rather, that we *haven't* received what we *have* deserved. All of us have been shown much more mercy than we've ever deserved—just like the people of ancient Egypt.

When suffering man says, "What have I done to deserve this?" he is revealing his inherent pride. He should be asking, "Why have I gotten off so easily?"

When the water turned to blood in Egypt, no Egyptian could justifiably say, "What have we done to deserve this?" Only two questions would have been justifiable in God's ears: "Why has God been so good to delay this present judgment for so many years?" and "Why is it that now, when God's judgment has fallen, we haven't received the fullness of what we really deserve?"

In truth, the Egyptians should have been confessing, "We have been so selfish, but we thank God for all the mercy He has shown us for so many years. And we appreciate His warning us of eternal judgment by means of this present judgment. Now we know that if we don't repent, we will ultimately get *everything* we deserve."

No one, ever, has any right to be angry with God.

Asking the Right Question

During one of His teachings, Jesus mentioned two contemporary tragedies that clearly present, from God's standpoint, what our attitude toward suffering should be—especially when it seems unjust:

> Now on the same occasion there were some present who reported to Him [Jesus] about the Galileans, whose blood Pilate had mingled with their sacrifices. And He answered and said to them, "Do you suppose that these Galileans were greater sinners than all other Galileans,

because they suffered this fate? I tell you, no, but, unless you repent, you will all likewise perish. Or do you suppose that those eighteen on whom the tower in Siloam fell and killed them, were worse culprits than all the men who live in Jerusalem? I tell you, no, but unless you repent, you will all likewise perish" (Luke 13:1-5).

Jesus said that those who died in the two tragedies He mentioned were sinners, but no greater sinners than anyone else. The sinners who died received what they deserved. The sinners who were still alive hadn't yet received what they deserved. They were mercifully being given time to repent. And if they didn't repent, they, too, would get what they deserved.

Jesus' listeners, just like people today, were asking the wrong question. Rather than asking, *"I wonder what those men did to deserve to die?"* they should have been asking, *"I wonder why I am still alive?"*

If we will be honest and view ourselves as God does, then the proper question we should all be asking is: "Why have I not suffered more for my selfishness?" Actually, an even more appropriate question would be, *"Why am I not burning in hell right now?"*

The answer, of course, is that God has shown all of us undeserved mercy. When we question God's fairness, our pride is unmasked. We think we deserve better treatment, and surely God must groan.

People often ask, "Why do bad things happen to good people?" A better question, asked from a truer perspective, would be, "Why does *anything* good happen to *anyone*?" According to Jesus, *no one* is good except God alone (see Mark 10:18). None of us are good; thus we all deserve only bad.

Jesus continued His lesson on God's undeserved mercy with the following words:

And He began telling them this parable: "A certain man had a fig tree which had been planted in his vineyard; and he came looking for fruit on it, and did not find any. And he said to the vineyard-keeper, 'Behold, for three years I have come looking for fruit on this fig tree without finding any. Cut it down! Why does it even use up the ground?' And he answered and said to him, 'Let it alone, sir, for this year too, until I dig around it and put in fertilizer; and if it bears fruit next year, fine; but if not, cut it down'" (Luke 13:6-9).

Here is a perfect picture of the justice and mercy of God. The fruitless fig tree deserved to be cut down but was shown mercy for one more year in the hope that it would bear fruit. If it bore no fruit on the fourth year, it would be cut down. When that time arrived, the question wouldn't be, "Why is it being cut down?" but "Why wasn't it cut down last year?" The answer is—because the tree was shown undeserved mercy.

Israel's Undeserved Mercy

How about the people of Israel? Did they deserve, because of their holiness, to be released from Egyptian bondage? No, the people of Israel were no doubt selfish in their dealings with others. They certainly weren't as cruel as the Egyptians, but neither did they lead lives of self-sacrificing service to one another. We know for certain that Moses once attempted to stop a fight between two Israelites (see Exodus 2:13).

Furthermore, certain Jewish tradition states that the reason God permitted Israel to become enslaved to Egypt was because of their sins. Beyond that, numerous times after their deliverance from Egypt, the people of Israel displayed traits of selfishness and greed (see Numbers 11:4, 31-34, 12:1-10, 14:1-4, 16:1-3).

So why did God free them? Was their suffering over the years—the death of their little babies, the hardships of their labor— sufficient payment for their sins? Had they received everything they deserved? Was God obligated to release them because their accounts with Him were all settled? Emphatically no.

And if God made anything clear on the night of the exodus, He made it clear to Israel that they were receiving undeserved mercy.

On the very day before the midnight exodus, God commanded that each Israelite family was to take a one year-old lamb and kill it at twilight. Then they were to take some of the blood from their lamb and smear it on the doorposts and lintels of their houses. God had said on that night He would pass through Egypt and kill all their first-born. But, when He saw the blood on the Israelites' doorposts, He promised to pass over them. Thus, they would escape His judgment.

This, of course, was the first Jewish Feast of Passover. Christians celebrate Easter at the same time of year, and rightfully so, as we will soon see.

What was the significance of the Passover ceremony? First of all, God commanded that each family take a one-year-old lamb—not a full-grown sheep but a white and fluffy baby lamb who was the picture of innocence—and slit its throat.

It sounds a little barbaric, especially to those of us who are only familiar with buying a leg of lamb at the grocery store. As we're enjoying our meal, we'd rather not think about how that little lamb had to be slaughtered before it was cooked.

Why would God command such a thing? If something had to be killed, why not an old ground hog or a worn-out pig? Why an innocent little lamb?

God was teaching Israel the principle of *representative substitution*. That is, the innocent dying for the sins of the guilty. *The lamb was chosen because it exemplified innocence.* It was killed because it was receiving what each Israelite deserved—death. And the blood that was smeared on the doorposts protected those within the house from the due wrath of God, obliging it to "pass over." The blood indicated that justice had already been executed on behalf of those inside.

The Perfect Sacrifice

How could the death of a lamb justly pay for the sins of a man? The answer is that *it couldn't*. In fact, the New Testament teaches it is impossible for the blood of animals to take away sins (see Hebrews 10:4).

Those little lambs only served to *represent* the Perfect Sacrifice that would one day completely satisfy the claims of divine justice on behalf of all men.

That Perfect Sacrifice couldn't be an animal, but a man. Only a man's death could justly recompense for a man's sins.

That man had to be sinless, perfectly innocent, without selfishness. A sin-stained man could never atone for the sins of others because he himself would be a debtor to God.

That man who would be the Perfect Sacrifice would have to be divine for only God is sinless.

That man was Jesus Christ.

It was Jesus who the angel announced to Joseph would "save His people from their sins" (Matthew 1:21).

It was Jesus who John the Baptist introduced as "the Lamb of God who takes away the sin of the world" (John 1:29).

It was Jesus who the apostle Paul declared was "our Passover" (1 Corinthians 5:7).

It was Jesus who willfully walked to Jerusalem and who was crucified *during the Passover Feast* there in 32 A.D.

That event was the culmination of God's foreordained plan to provide a means whereby self-condemned men and women could escape the due wrath of God. On that day divine justice was executed upon a willing sinless substitute. Now undeserving sinners could justly be offered eternal mercy from God.

It was Jesus' death on the cross that fulfilled what every

Passover lamb's death for over a thousand years only fore-shadowed: the ransom price for man's deliverance from God's wrath had been paid in full.

When Jesus cried out from the cross with His last breath, "It is finished!" our salvation was purchased, once and for all. This is the central theme of the Bible.

Turning Away God's Wrath

Too many have thought the purpose for Jesus' coming was to "show us how to live." Others think His death was just another unfortunate case of a good person being martyred for a worthy cause. Certainly Jesus did teach us how to live, and yes, He died for a worthy cause. But the foremost reason Jesus came to earth was to give His life as payment for our sins.

Jesus was born to die.

He knew that and proclaimed it:

> "For even the Son of Man did not come to be served, but to serve, *and to give His life a ransom for many*" (Jesus—Mark 10:45; italics mine).

This was God's foreordained plan. Seven hundred years before Jesus was born in Bethlehem, the prophet Isaiah predicted His arrival and the purpose for His coming:

> But He was pierced through for our transgressions, He was crushed for our iniquities; the chastening for our well-being fell upon Him, and by His scourging we are healed. All of us like sheep have gone astray, each one of us to our own way; but *the Lord has caused the iniquity of us all to fall on Him....*[He] will justify the many, as He will bear their iniquities (Isaiah 53:5-6, 11b; italics mine).

The apostle Paul wrote that Jesus' sacrificial death as our substitute is the most important spiritual truth of the Christian faith:

> For I delivered to you as of *first importance* what I also received, that *Christ died for our sins according to the Scriptures...* (1 Corinthians 15:3; italics mine).

One biblical term used to describe Jesus' work on the cross is *propitiation*. It means "to turn away wrath." The apostle John explained that God's love was preeminently demonstrated through the *propitiatory* work of His Son:

> By this the love of God was manifested in us, that God has sent His only begotten Son into the world so that we might live through Him. In this is love, not that we loved God, but that He loved us and sent His Son to be the *propitiation* for our sins (1 John 4:9-10; italics mine).

The principal benefit that Jesus' sacrifice makes available to us is the turning away of God's wrath (see Romans 5:9). That in turn, makes available a multitude of other blessings to every person who receives the reconciliation God has made possible.

Does Jesus' sacrificial death automatically guarantee that every person will escape hell and live forever in heaven? No, every person must meet certain requirements if he is to experience what Christ made possible.

Notice the scripture below states that even though Jesus' death has provided our reconciliation with God, we have a responsibility to *receive* that reconciliation:

> For while we were still helpless, at the right time Christ died for the ungodly. For one will hardly die for a righteous man; though perhaps for the good man someone would dare even to die. But God demonstrates His own love toward us, in that while we were yet sinners, Christ died for us. Much more then, having now been justified by His blood, *we shall be saved from the wrath of God through Him.* For if while we were enemies, we

were reconciled to God through the death of His Son, much more, having been reconciled, we shall be saved by His life. And not only this, but we also exult in God through our Lord Jesus Christ, *through whom we have now received the reconciliation* (Romans 5:6-11; italics mine).

How do we receive the reconciliation that has been provided? In the next chapter I'll answer that question, as we examine what God requires of every man.

The Demonstration of the Cross

In Jesus' death on the cross, we see God's holiness, His justice, and His love perfectly blended into one event. God's love was demonstrated in that Jesus died in *our* stead, so we wouldn't suffer our due punishment.

Jesus said, "Greater love has no one than this, that one lay down his life for his friends" (John 15:13). How could God have demonstrated greater love?

God's justice was demonstrated in that He didn't pardon us without punishment. If He would have, He could be rightly accused of injustice, and, therefore, imperfect in love and immoral. So God meted out the due penalty—His wrath fell to the just degree—but upon a Sinless Substitute, who willingly went to the cross for us.

But how did God's wrath fall upon our Substitute?

First of all, God's wrath fell upon Jesus in the agony of scourging and crucifixion.

As blood streamed down His face from the puncture wounds of a crown of thorns pressed into His head, the flesh of Jesus' back was lacerated to shreds by the Roman cat-o´-nine-tails. Each leather strand of that whip was tipped with pieces of metal and sharp bones that imbedded themselves and tore without mercy. They each ripped into Jesus' back *thirty-nine times*. History records that weaker men died just from the scourging.

Jesus was then forced to carry His own cross upon His bleeding back until He dropped to His knees from exhaustion. At the crucifixion site, the executioners stripped Him naked and stretched out His arms that were already splattered with blood. With cruel precision they hammered heavy nails through His wrists and both His feet.

Finally the cross upon which He was impaled was lifted up and dropped into a supporting hole that would keep it standing upright.

In crucifixion, all of the victim's weight rested on the place where the nail went through his feet and where the nails went through his wrists. The pain, of course, was excruciating. Breathing became a constant struggle. If the condemned wanted a breath, he'd have to push up on the nail through his feet in order to relax the tremendous cramping pressure his body weight placed upon his lungs.

It would have been even worse for one whose back was lacerated from scourging. The cross would have scraped the already gapping wounds as the victim pushed up for a breath and, then, collapsing in agony, slid back down the cross, once more hanging from his hands.

Most who were crucified died of asphyxiation, since they were eventually unable to muster the strength to push up and get one more breath. The two thieves who were crucified on either side of Jesus had their legs broken in order to accelerate their deaths.

Jesus had been so abused beforehand that there was no need to break His legs—He was dead after only a few hours on the cross.

Forsaken For You

The torture of the crucifixion is almost too horrible to imagine, but Jesus suffered infinitely more and in a way that is inconceivable to our human minds.

God's wrath fell upon Jesus and inflicted much greater pain and suffering than the physical torment of the cross. All the guilt of the human race—for all of the hatred, the lust, the envy, the pride, the selfishness—was placed upon Jesus.

In dreadful anticipation of this punishment, Jesus had fallen on His face and fervently prayed that if it were possible, to let the cup pass from Him. But rather than say "Amen," He added, "Yet not My will, but Thine be done" (Luke 22:42).

We cannot begin to understand the agony Jesus experienced on the cross—as the torments of an eternal hell were compressed into three hours and laid upon one single man. He felt the intense loneliness, the hopelessness and despair, the guilt, the regret, the horror, the raging thirst, of those who suffer the never-ending torments of the damned.

Worst of all, He felt the panic of those who realize there is no hope for their reconciliation with God, abandoned forever, cast into outer darkness. As the crushing reality of being abandoned by His Father crescendoed within His consciousness, Jesus gasped with horror,

"My God, My God, Why hast Thou forsaken Me?"

His own Father had turned His back upon Him and poured out His fury until His wrath was spent—until Jesus' body hung limp on the cross.

There hung the Lamb of God. Beaten, kicked, spit upon, mocked, scourged, stripped, impaled, and covered with dirt, sweat and blood.

That is how much God hates selfishness. That is how just and righteous God is. And that is how much God loves you.

§

SEVEN

Opening the Door

Are you ready to respond to what God, through His Son Jesus, has done for you—now that you understand why He had to die on the cross?

Maybe you're wondering, "What could I ever do to make myself worthy to possess the benefits made available by Jesus' suffering? Should I climb some high mountain on my bare knees? Would living a life of solitary confinement as a monk make me worthy? What if I promise to go to church every day? Would that be enough?"

The answer to those questions may surprise you: There is absolutely *nothing* you can do to make yourself worthy to receive God's forgiveness.

This is the message of Jesus' cross: Sinful man doesn't have a shadow of a chance of obtaining right standing with God through his own merit. Why? Because man's entire life is characterized by selfishness.

The only hope man has of being saved from his due

punishment is if somehow God pardons him. Jesus' sacrificial death provides the means whereby God can justly forgive our sins. Jesus willingly took our punishment for us.

Salvation is the work of God—not man.

We can have our sins forgiven only because of His *mercy*. To think that we can even partially merit what God has freely offered us is a prideful assault against the necessity of Jesus' terrible suffering and God's undeserved mercy upon us.

What Must We Do?

How do we receive the benefit of what God has made available to us through Jesus Christ?

In the Bible, there are two requirements listed: repentance and faith. Neither of these can make us worthy, but together they open the door for God's salvation to become effective in our lives.

Let's first examine repentance.

Most of us, when we hear the word "repent," think of some wild-eyed, back-woods preacher who self-righteously rides into town to condemn the sins of the townsfolk. His message is never well received because he only preaches about sin and the coming judgment. His hearers are left with the impression that if they can just straighten out their lives and obtain a certain standard of holy living, then they can earn their place in glory.

I hope you realize that this kind of message is gravely inadequate in portraying a true picture of God's plan for mankind. Telling sinners to clean up their lives without mention of Jesus' death on the cross is a crime.

Still, the Bible makes it clear that repentance is absolutely necessary for salvation. A person can never hope to experience forgiveness from God unless He repents. On the other hand, repentance in itself could never save anyone. Repentance must be joined with faith.

Because the necessity of repentance for salvation has been

played down in some theological circles, I'm going to take a few pages to prove that you can't be saved from God's wrath with repenting. Then I'll discuss exactly what it means to repent.

First Things First

John the Baptist, Jesus' forerunner, preached a very simple message:

> "*Repent*, for the kingdom of God is at hand" (Matthew 3:2; italics mine).

The Bible says that from the time Jesus first began preaching, His message was the same as John the Baptist's:

> From that time Jesus began to preach and say, "*Repent*, for the kingdom of heaven is at hand" (Matthew 4:17; italics mine).

You probably remember the scripture I quoted in the previous chapter concerning Jesus' comments about two contemporary tragedies. Referring to the men who had died, Jesus twice told His listeners:

> "I tell you...*unless you repent*, you will all likewise perish" (Luke 13:3, 5; italics mine).

When Jesus sent out His twelve disciples to preach in various cities, what was the message they preached? The Bible says:

> And they went out and preached that men should *repent* (Mark 6:12; italics mine).

What was the message Jesus told the twelve to take with them after His resurrection?

> And He said to them, "Thus it is written, that the Christ should suffer and rise again from the dead on the third

day; and that *repentance* for forgiveness of sins should be proclaimed in His name to all the nations, beginning from Jerusalem" (Lk. 24:46-47; italics mine).

The apostles obeyed Jesus' instructions. When the apostle Peter was preaching on the day of Pentecost, his convicted listeners, after realizing the truth about the Man whom they had recently crucified, asked Peter what they should do. His response was that they, first of all, should repent (see Acts 2:38).

Peter's second sermon at Solomon's portico contained the identical message:

> "*Repent* therefore and return, that your sins may be wiped away..." (Acts 3:19a; italics mine).

Did the apostle Paul preach repentance? Decidedly yes. In Athens we hear him proclaim:

> "Therefore having overlooked the times of ignorance, God is now declaring to men that *all everywhere should repent,* because He has fixed a day in which He will judge the world in righteousness through a Man whom He has appointed, having furnished proof to all men by raising Him from the dead" (Acts 17:30-31; italics mine).

In his farewell sermon to the Ephesian elders, Paul stated:

> "...I did not shrink from...solemnly testifying to both Jews and Greeks of *repentance* toward God and faith in our Lord Jesus Christ" (Acts 20:20a, 21; italics mine).

In his defense before King Agrippa, Paul said:

> "Consequently, King Agrippa, I did not prove disobedient to the heavenly vision, but kept declaring both to those of Damascus first, and also at Jerusalem and then throughout the region of Judea, and even to the Gentiles,

that they should *repent* and turn to God, performing *deeds appropriate to repentance"* (Acts 26:19-20; italics mine).

The writer of the book of Hebrews said that "repentance from dead works" is the most fundamental doctrine of Christ (see Heb. 6:1).

Hopefully, that list of scriptural proofs is enough to convince anyone that a relationship with God begins with repentance. *There is no forgiveness of sins without it.*

What Does Repentance Mean?

If repentance is a necessity for salvation, it is of utmost importance that we understand what it means to repent. Actually, once we understand that all sin basically stems from selfishness—and once we realize that Jesus died for us because of our sins—then the definition of repentance becomes obvious. *To repent means to turn from sin and selfishness.*

Repentance requires more than just a change of mind on our part. It necessitates a change in our actions. It requires that we stop living for ourselves and begin living for others.

If the reason we were formerly separated *from* God was because of our rebellious acts of sin, then naturally repentance would be required if we plan to begin a relationship *with* Him.

John the Baptist, whose message was one that called people to repentance, couldn't have made more clear what repentance involves. Clearly, repentance requires *action.* Listen to what he preached:

"Therefore *bring forth fruits in keeping with your repentance,* and do not begin to say to yourselves, 'We have Abraham for our father,' for I say to you that God is able from these stones to raise up children to Abraham. And also the axe is already laid at the root of the trees; *every*

> *tree therefore that does not bear good fruit is cut down and thrown into the fire"* (Luke 3:8-9; italics mine).

True repentance will bring forth fruit, or actions. Notice also that John the Baptist declared that people who don't repent go to hell. Let's continue:

> And the multitudes were questioning him, saying, "Then what shall we do?" And he would answer and say to them, "Let the man who has two tunics share with him who has none; and let him who has food do likewise" (Luke 3:10-11).

Repentance affects what we do with our possessions and makes us compassionate toward the less fortunate.
John continued:

> And some tax-gatherers also came to be baptized, and they said to him, "Teacher, what shall we do?" And he said to them, "Collect no more than what you have been ordered to" (Luke 3:12-13).

Repentance affects our honesty with our employer and our clients.
John concluded:

> And some soldiers were questioning him, saying, "And what about us, what shall we do?" And he said to them, "Do not take money from anyone by force, or accuse anyone falsely, and be content with your wages" (Luke 3:14).

Repentance affects our consideration for others and curbs our greed.
Can you see that repentance requires a change of attitudes and actions? And did you notice that everything John told his inquirers to do could be summed up in the words, "Stop being selfish"?

If true repentance takes place, then we will no longer be motivated by selfish ambition but by love for others. *The identifying mark of the Christian ought to be unselfish love for others.* (See also Acts 26:20, which affirms that repentance involves not only a change of mind but also a change of actions.)

The Little Man Who Truly Repented

There is a story in the Bible of a short man named Zaccheus who was a tax-gatherer. You must understand that in Palestine in Jesus' day, the words *tax-gatherer* and *swindler* were synonymous terms. The Roman government sold the right to collect taxes to the highest bidder, and the more money the tax-gatherer collected, the more money he could keep for himself. Human nature being what it was and *is* (selfish), tax-collectors normally defrauded a lot of tax-paying people.

Zaccheus was a normal tax-gatherer: dishonest and wealthy. Let's read his story:

And He [Jesus] entered and was passing through Jericho. And behold, there was a man called by the name of Zaccheus; and he was a chief tax-gatherer, and he was rich. And he was trying to see who Jesus was, and he was unable because of the crowd, for he was small in stature. And he ran on ahead and climbed up into a sycamore tree in order to see Him, for He was about to pass through that way.

And when Jesus came to the place, He looked up and said to him, "Zaccheus, hurry and come down, for today I must stay at your house." And he hurried and came down, and received Him gladly.

And when they saw it, they all began to grumble, saying, "He has gone to be the guest of a man who is a sinner." [Of course, none of those grumblers ever acted in their own self-interest, did they?] And Zaccheus stopped and said to the Lord, "Behold, Lord, half of my possessions I will give to the poor, and if I have defrauded anyone of anything, I will give back four times as much."

And Jesus said to him, "Today salvation has come to this house, because he, too, is a son of Abraham. For the Son of Man has come to seek and to save that which was lost" (Luke 19:1-10).

We know that Zaccheus repented. His actions made it evident. Jesus must have been convinced because He said that salvation had come to the tax collector's house that day—the day he repented.

If we truly repent, we must stop taking selfish advantage of other people. It's one thing to make money by charging reasonable fees for quality goods and services but another thing to make money by ripping people off.

It was selfishness that motivated Zaccheus to be greedy and dishonest. It was the love of Jesus that motivated him to repent.

So if you want to meet the first requirement to be saved from God's wrath, then *repent*. Any acts of selfishness of which you are conscious should immediately be stopped. Pray and ask God's forgiveness for a life of selfishness. And if tears come, let them come.

Repentance doesn't make you worthy—it doesn't earn your salvation—only Jesus' death saves us. More than anything else, repentance proves that you are also meeting the second requirement, and that is to believe the gospel.

Repentance and faith go hand-in-hand. Just as Jesus Himself said, *"Repent,* and *believe* in the gospel"! (Mark 1:15; italics mine).

What is the Gospel?

The word "gospel" means "good news." That is what we

must believe.

What is the good news? That Jesus Christ, the sinless Son of God, has died on the cross, suffered as payment for our sins, averted the wrath of God that we deserved, and has risen from the dead to live forever.

If you have repented and truly believed that good news, you are saved. *You will not go to hell.* You are guaranteed a place in heaven, forever! Now that's something to get excited about! (Incidentally, the angels in heaven do get excited about it; see Luke 15:1-10).

Let's look at a few scriptures that tell us *faith in the gospel* is an absolute requirement for salvation. First, let's read probably the most well-known verse in the entire Bible, John 3:16:

> "For God so loved the world, that He gave His only begotten Son, that whoever *believes in Him* should not perish, but have eternal life" (italics mine).

This, of course, means more than just believing that Jesus was a historical person who walked on the earth 2,000 years ago. To believe in Him means to believe in *who He is and what He has accomplished*: He is the Son of God, and His death paid the price for our sins. If you believe that, you are saved. You have eternal life.

Throughout the New Testament scriptures, we are promised that if we believe certain essential elements of the gospel, we will be saved. Fundamentally, we must believe that Jesus is the Son of God. Because if He isn't God's Son, then He was sin-stained like everyone else and, therefore, wasn't qualified to be our substitute. A man on death-row could never offer his life to pay the penalty for another inmate on death-row! Why? Because he owes his *own* life! Only One who is sinless could be our rightful substitute.

In the book of Acts, Philip the evangelist wouldn't baptize an Ethiopian eunuch until he confessed his faith that Jesus

Christ was the Son of God:

> And Philip opened his mouth, and beginning from this
> scripture he preached Jesus to him. And as they went
> along the road they came to some water; and the eunuch
> said, "Look! Water! What prevents me from being
> baptized?" And Philip said, "If you believe with all your
> heart, you may." And he answered, *"I believe that Jesus
> Christ is the Son of God."* And he ordered the chariot to
> stop; and they both went down into the water...and he
> baptized him (Acts 8:35-38; italics mine).

Of course, it's one thing to say you believe that Jesus is the
Son of God, and another thing to actually believe it. Many
people have said that they believe Jesus is the Son of God, but
it is obvious that they really don't. Why? If a person truly
believes that Jesus is the Son of God, then he will *act* as if he
does.

If I really believe that Jesus is the Son of God, then I will
be interested in learning what Jesus has said. I will realize that
He has a right to tell me how to live my life, and I will want
to obey Him.

Once a person really believes that Jesus is the Son of God,
he'll repent. As I've already stated, repentance and faith go
hand in hand. If you truly believe, you will repent. Your
actions will prove your faith.

Not only must we believe that Jesus is the Son of God, but
we must also believe that He died for our sins. It was His
death that makes our salvation possible. As the apostle Paul
stated:

> Now I make known to you, brethren, the gospel which
> I preached to you, which also you received, in which also
> you stand, by which also you are saved....For I delivered
> to you as of first importance what I also received, that
> *Christ died for our sins according to the Scriptures...* (1
> Corinthians 15:1-3; italics mine).

If we believe that Jesus died in our place, we will naturally *want* to repent of our selfishness. We won't desire to live for ourselves any longer; we'll want to live for Jesus:

> For the love of Christ controls us, having concluded this, that one died for all, therefore all died ["all" refers to us; because of Jesus' suffering for all people, God imputes His death to our account]; and He died for all, *that they who live should no longer live for themselves, but for Him who died and rose again on their behalf* (2 Corinthians 5:14-15; italics mine).

Finally, as the above scripture also states, we must believe that *Jesus rose from the dead.* Jesus' resurrection is the ultimate proof that the penalty for our sins has been paid in full and that God's wrath has been turned away for all those who will believe in Jesus.

Furthermore, Jesus' resurrection proves that we, too, will live after we've died. Because He was our Substitute on the Cross, we are joined in vital union with Jesus through the working of God. Now that Jesus is alive, we will live forever, too:

> He who was delivered up because of our transgressions [sins], *and was raised because of our justification* [our sentence has been paid in full—now we have right-standing before God](Romans 4:25; italics mine).

> And if Christ has *not* been raised, your faith is worthless; you are still in your sins. Then those who have fallen asleep in Christ Jesus [those Christians who have died] have perished [in hell]....But now Christ *has* been raised from the dead, the first fruits of those who are asleep (I Corinthians 15:17-20; italics mine).

Do you truly believe that Jesus is the Son of God and that He died for your sins? Do you believe that Jesus' death fully averted the wrath of God that you deserved? Do you believe that Jesus Christ was raised from the dead?

Good! Your sins have all been forgiven; your guilt is wiped away; and you don't have to worry about getting the wrath of God you deserve! And you have a wonderful future to look forward to!

Can I be Certain I Will Go to Heaven?

So many people have never realized that it *is* possible to *know* for certain, while here on earth, that they will go to heaven when they die. When we repent and believe the gospel, we immediately have that assurance, as the apostle John expressed:

> These things I have written to you who believe in the name of the Son of God, in order that you may *know* that you have eternal life (1 John 5:13; italics mine).

The reason so many people don't think it's possible to have the assurance of eternal life is because they think their good deeds save them. Too many people are just hoping that they've done enough good things and not too many bad things, so they won't go to hell but to heaven.

The truth is, *no one* is good enough to get into heaven— it's impossible to earn that privilege, as I'm sure you've come to realize after reading the first six chapters of this book.

The Bible is crystal clear on this fact: *good works can't save us*. Only our *faith* can guarantee salvation. Our salvation is a free gift from God because of His love, His grace, and His mercy. Here are a few of the many scriptures which prove this point:

> For by grace [undeserved favor] *you have been saved through faith;* and that is not of yourselves, *it is the gift of God; not as a result of [good] works,* that no one should boast (Ephesians 2:8-9; italics mine).

> He saved us, *not on the basis of deeds which we have*

done in righteousness, but according to His mercy... (Titus 3:5a; italics mine).

...for all have sinned and fall short of the glory of God, being justified [made righteous before God] *as a gift by His grace* through the redemption which is in Christ Jesus; whom God displayed publicly as a *propitiation* in His blood through faith (Romans 3:23-25a; italics mine).

If it were possible for us to be saved by our own good works, then there was no need for Jesus to have died. As the apostle Paul said, His death would have been a waste of time:

I do not nullify the grace of God; for if righteousness [right standing with God] comes through the Law [keeping the Ten Commandments], then Christ died needlessly (Galatians 2:21).

Religious or Righteous?

Possibly you've heard the story that Jesus told about the Pharisee and the publican. The Pharisees in Jesus' day were super-religious, and they lived by a strict code of man-made laws. The word *publican* is another word for *tax-gatherer*, which hopefully you remember was synonymous with the word *swindler* in Jesus' day.

The story of the Pharisee and the publican perfectly illustrates that those who trust in their own good works will not be saved. But those who admit their sinfulness and come to God in faith, trusting in Jesus' death, *will* be saved:

And He also told this parable to certain ones who trusted in themselves that they were righteous, and viewed others with contempt:

"Two men went up into the temple to pray, one a Pharisee, and the other a tax-gatherer. The Pharisee stood and was praying thus to himself, 'God, I thank

Thee that I am not like other people; swindlers, unjust, adulterers, or even like this tax-gatherer. I fast twice a week; I pay tithes of all that I get.' But the tax-gatherer, standing some distance away, was even unwilling to lift his eyes to heaven, but was beating his breast, saying, 'God, be merciful to me, the sinner!'

"I tell you, this man went down to his house justified [made righteous with God] rather than the other; for every one who exults himself shall be humbled, but he who humbles himself shall be exalted" (Luke 18:9-14).

Notice the tax-gatherer prayed, "Lord, be *merciful* to me, the sinner!" Literally, the original Greek translation says, "Lord, be *propitious* to me...!" Do you remember what *propitiate* means? It means "to avert anger" or "to turn away wrath."

God's wrath cannot be withheld if He is to remain perfectly loving and perfectly just. So God's wrath wasn't withheld—but it was redirected *at Jesus.* And that is how we escaped getting what we deserved. Our salvation is free to us but not to Jesus—it cost Him unimaginable suffering.

When a person attempts to save himself by his own good deeds, he is pridefully declaring that he doesn't need Jesus because he can be his own savior. Furthermore, he is unconsciously voicing his opinion that Jesus was a fool since He endured such suffering for no good reason. Such a person also thinks the Creator must have been confused when He planned the culminating event of all history—the death of His only begotten Son on Calvary.

Without overstatement, the idea that man can save himself is the most damnable heresy ever invented by man, and stands in direct opposition to everything the Bible teaches, everything that true Christianity represents, and everything that the all-wise and all-loving God has planned for mankind. Amen!

A Sinner's Prayer for Salvation

It would be best if you prayed to God from your own heart, using your own words, as you repent and declare your faith in Jesus. But if you are having a difficult time talking to God, here is a prayer you could use, as long as you pray it from your heart. Pray aloud:

Oh God, I admit that I am a guilty sinner who deserves to receive your just punishment. Thank you for warning me of the ultimate consequences of my sin so that I can avoid spending an eternity in hell. I've been selfish, but today I repent, and my change of actions will prove it. I believe that Jesus Christ is the Son of God, that He died on the cross for my sins, that He has averted the wrath of God that I deserve, and that He rose again from the grave. He is Lord, and from now on He is my Lord, whom I will obey. I do not trust that any of my own good deeds will save me but that my salvation stems solely from what Jesus has done on the cross. From this day on, He is my Savior. Thank you for saving me! In Jesus name, Amen.

§

EIGHT

Rebirth

I wonder if the drab caterpillar, as he spins his cocoon, understands what is about to happen to him. Does he labor instinctively, uncomprehending, or is he looking forward with excitement to becoming a new and improved creature? Is it because he envisions himself as a beautiful butterfly that he toils so hard? Of course, no one knows what the caterpillar might be thinking.

Regardless, the caterpillar is a prime example of God's power to change something mundane into something exquisitely beautiful. Once limited to slowly crawling down one plant and up another, now the butterfly can fly to exotic destinations and do it in style. Once unnoticed and uncomplimented, he is now praised by on-lookers for his delicate beauty as he flutters by. Once at risk of being squashed by uncaring children, now he has become their elusive prize. Once disdained, now he competes with flowers.

Is it possible for God to recreate a human being, change him from a guilt-ridden, sin-sick, selfish creature, into one who radiates love, who lives in harmony with his fellowman, who finds his greatest joy in serving others?

Not only is it possible, but God has already begun that process in *you*. Your metamorphosis is one that begins on the inside and then manifests itself on the outside. Jesus unveiled the marvels of that potential human transformation in one of His conversations with a man named Nicodemus:

> Now there was a man of the Pharisees, named Nicodemus, a ruler of the Jews; this man came to Him by night, and said to Him, "Rabbi, we know that You have come from God as a teacher; for no one can do these signs that You do unless God is with Him."
>
> Jesus answered and said to him, "Truly, truly, I say to you, unless one is born again, he cannot see the kingdom of God."
>
> Nicodemus said to Him, "How can a man be born when he is old? He cannot enter a second time into his mother's womb and be born, can he?"
>
> Jesus answered, "Truly, truly, I say to you, unless one is born of water and the Spirit, he cannot enter the kingdom of God. That which is born of the flesh is flesh; and that which is born of the Spirit is spirit. Do not marvel that I said to you, 'You must be born again.' The wind blows where it wishes and you hear the sound of it, but do not know where it comes from and where it is going; so is everyone who is born of the Spirit" (John 3:1-8).

Notice Jesus said that it is *impossible* to enter the kingdom of God without being born again. He went on to explain to Nicodemus that one is born again when he places his faith in Jesus and what He did on the cross (see John 3:14-16). If you have done that, then you, my dear friend, have been born again!

Jesus originally coined the term, *born again*, but, unfortunately, it has been worn out from overuse in our society. The pure meaning of the phrase has now become polluted as everyone talks about his "born-again experience"—whether it be because of finding a new wife or tasting a new breakfast cereal.

Jesus, however, was talking about a rebirth that is significant—no one can enter heaven unless they've experienced it. This rebirth is one that is *spiritual*. We who have believed in Jesus have literally experienced a spiritual rebirth. Let's examine this truth.

The Hidden You

The Bible teaches that every person is more than just a body containing a brain, bones, and muscle. According to the Word of God, we are tripartite in nature—spirit, soul, and body. The apostle Paul made this clear in his benediction to the Christians of Thessalonica:

> Now may the God of peace Himself sanctify you entirely; and may your *spirit* and *soul* and *body* be preserved complete, without blame at the coming of our Lord Jesus (1 Thessalonians 5:23; italics mine).

Obviously your body is what you can see in the mirror. Your soul is your mind, emotions, and intellect. But modern man has only faint visages of the human spirit, labeling it the "subconscious." It remains largely hidden from human understanding. God's Word, however, unveils exactly what the human spirit is—that isn't surprising since God is the one who places a spirit within each man.

Jesus said that God is a spirit (see John 4:24). That doesn't mean He is just an impersonal force or some nebulous cloud. Jesus said that God has a form (see John 5:37), and we have been created in His image. God, however, is not comprised of flesh and blood but of "spiritual material." Of course, we can only comprehend that to a certain degree.

We, too, are spiritual beings and just like God, our spirits have a shape or form. In fact, your spirit has the same general shape as your body. The Bible refers to the human spirit as "the inward man." For example, the apostle Paul states:

...though our outer man is decaying, yet our *inner man* is being renewed day by day (2 Corinthians 4:16; italics mine).

Paul said we have an *outer man* and an *inner man*. The outer man is the body, which is decaying or getting older, and the inner man is our spirit. Again, notice that the spirit is referred to as a *man*. The inner man is not getting any older because he is eternal. He will live forever, and is, therefore, as Paul says, being "renewed day by day."

The apostle Peter refers to the spirit as "the hidden person of the heart" (1 Pet. 3:4). Again, the spirit is called a "person" who is hidden. Your spirit is a person. Your spirit is the *real* you. In one sense, your body is only a container in which your spirit temporarily lives. When your body dies, your spirit lives on, traveling to one of two places: heaven or hell.

The Rebirth of the Spirit

When Jesus had His conversation with Nicodemus and told him that he needed to be born again, Nicodemus immediately thought of a physical rebirth: "How can a man be born when he is old? He cannot enter a second time into his mother's womb and be born, can he?" (John 3:4)

Jesus cleared up Nicodemus' thinking by saying that it isn't a physical rebirth that is required for entrance into heaven but a spiritual rebirth: "That which is born of the flesh is flesh; and that which is born of the Spirit is spirit" (John 3:6).

When we repent and believe the gospel, it is our spirits that are reborn by the direct action of God's Spirit. The amazing changes that take place at salvation are internal rather than external. But those inward changes will manifest themselves outwardly, just as Jesus went on to say: "The wind blows where it wishes and you hear the sound of it, but do not know where it is going; so is everyone who is born of the Spirit" (John 3:8).

Although the wind can't be seen, it's obvious when it arrives because leaves rustle and branches bend. The same is true of the rebirth of the human spirit. When a person is reborn, you can't see with your physical eyes what has transpired in his invisible spirit. But you can see the evidence of it in his lifestyle. More than anything else, that person's life will begin to be characterized by unselfish love.

In fact, that's the reason one of those born-again people gave you this book! He or she loves you and is more concerned with your eternal destiny than with his or her own reputation.

One of the preeminent ways to determine if a person has been truly reborn by God's Spirit is if he displays a concern for the eternal destiny of others. You probably have already sensed the urge to share what you have recently learned with those who don't know it yet. But before you give this book away, make sure you finish the remaining chapters!

Being Born Into God's Family

Amazingly, when our spirits are reborn by God's Spirit, we actually become children of God Himself. Our spirits are literally born of God, and He becomes our Heavenly Father. There is no greater Bible truth than this!:

> For you are all *sons of God* through faith in Christ Jesus....See how great a love the Father has bestowed upon us, that we should be called *children of God*; and such we are....Beloved, now we are the *children of God* (Galatians 3:26, 1 John 3:1-2; italics mine).

91

Furthermore, when we are born again, God's Spirit comes to live inside us:

> Or do you not know that your body is a temple of the Holy Spirit who is in you, whom you have from God...? (1 Corinthians 6:19).

God's Spirit, the Holy Spirit, is the third divine Person of the Trinity. Therefore, we can say that God Himself, by the Holy Spirit, has come to live in us! I know that sounds amazing, and it is! But we shouldn't be surprised because Jesus Himself promised us:

> "And I will ask the Father, and He will give you another Helper, that He may be with you forever; that is the Spirit of truth, whom the world [those who are unsaved] cannot receive, because it does not behold Him or know Him, but you know Him because He abides with you, and *will be in you*" (John 14:16-17; italics mine).

Notice that the Holy Spirit is not an "it" but is referred to by using the personal pronoun *Him*. He is a person. He is God. And He lives in you. But this is only true for those who have placed their faith in Jesus. No one else has God's Spirit living on the inside of them.

Naturally, if God comes to live inside you, then there is going to be a change in your life. If God is love, then it would be impossible for God to live inside you apart from His love. Therefore, we can say with assurance that God's love has been deposited within your spirit. This concurs with Scripture:

> ...the love of God has been poured out within our hearts through the Holy Spirit who was given to us (Romans 5:5).

So you see that if you've repented and believed in Jesus, God has done much more for you than simply forgiven your sins! He's declared you righteous and treats you as if you've never sinned. In addition, He has caused you to be spiritually reborn so that you are now His child. God has given you His Holy Spirit so that He Himself lives within you and has deposited a new nature of unselfish love in your spirit!

You belong to God and He belongs to you! You know, I think this is the beginning of a wonderful relationship!

§

"Therefore if any man is in Christ, he is a new creature; the old things passed away; behold, new things have come" (2 Corinthians 5:17).

NINE

Lord, Liar, or Lunatic?

H ave you ever heard anyone make this statement?:

> "I think that the idea of Jesus Christ is just a myth. The whole incredible story was just invented by a few religious zealots years ago, and consequently, multitudes of people have been deceived."

That's what people sometimes say when you begin to talk to them about Jesus Christ. They imagine He's in the same category as Zeus, Hercules, and Pandora. However, the idea of Jesus being a myth is based solely upon the personal bias of the pseudo-intellectual person who makes such an absurd claim and not upon historical evidence.

It's a fact of history—a man named Jesus actually walked on this earth about 2,000 years ago, and anyone who denies it is revealing a willful ignorance of what every student of history knows cannot be intelligently denied. A person might as well claim that George Washington or Abraham Lincoln was a myth. Jesus was no myth. The *Encyclopaedia Britannica* contains over 20,000 words under the entry *Jesus Christ*!

How do we know for certain that Jesus was a historical person? Although we don't have a copy of His birth or death certificate or any photographs of Him, there is more than sufficient evidence to prove that He lived for thirty-three years on this planet. A number of non-Christian first century writers document the historicity of Jesus and the early Christians.

Besides those documents, the foremost historical proofs are the four biographies about Jesus: two of the gospel accounts were written by disciples who knew Him personally, and the other two were authored by men who were His contemporaries.

Good Fiction?

Some might claim that the gospels are simply imaginative fiction. But stop and think for a moment how ridiculous that theory is.

What if someone were to publish a book about former President Dwight Eisenhower and report within the book that Mr. Eisenhower worked many miracles during his lifetime—that he healed incurably sick people, raised the dead, multiplied food, and walked on water? Not only that, but Mr. Eisenhower claimed to be the Son of God and was murdered because of it. Then he miraculously rose from the dead three days after his death, fulfilling an event that he himself predicted would occur.

How many copies would such a book sell? How long would it take before it would be on the *New York Times* bestseller list? Of course, no one but a fool would buy such a book, knowing it was a historical farce. The author would be ridiculed or ignored.

Now what are the chances that four different authors could write widely accepted biographies of Jesus within a few years of His life, reporting His miracles, His claims to be the Son of God, and His resurrection? How could that happen if, in fact, He never lived or had lived just an ordinary life? Would anyone have believed their stories? Of course not.

Not only were the gospel accounts of Jesus' life believed, but they were revered and carefully hand copied over and over again. Within a few years they had been translated into other languages, so that today we possess *thousands* of ancient manuscripts that contain portions of the New Testament (and in some cases *all* of the New Testament) that date between 130 A.D. to 400 A.D.

Compare those figures with the works of Aristotle, who wrote 350 years before Christ. The most ancient copies we have of his works are a few dated 1,100 A.D.—1,400 years *after* he wrote the originals!

Who Saw What Happened?

It would have been quite simple for anyone to discredit all four gospel accounts if they were indeed false, especially in light of the *incredible* events that each author reported. But the truth is, no one could successfully discredit their accounts because there were *thousands* of people who could substantiate the authenticity of their facts.

Thousands of people had seen Jesus; thousands had heard Him preach; thousands were miraculously healed by Him; thousands had eaten food that He multiplied; thousands had witnessed His crucifixion; and we know that *at least* 500 people saw Him after He had risen from the dead (see 1 Corinthians 15:6)

The biographies of Jesus that Matthew, Mark, Luke, and John wrote were accepted by a wide audience. Why? Because much of what they wrote was common knowledge to multitudes of people.

Do we have any further proof that Jesus actually lived? How about the fact that many of the people who agreed with the truth of the four gospels were willing to die for their beliefs. Ten of Jesus' twelve disciples died the death of martyrs. Would those men have died for something they knew was just a lie? Of course not.

It has been estimated that as many as *six million* people gave their lives as martyrs during the three centuries after Jesus' life. Would all of those people have died for someone who couldn't be proven historically to have existed?

Getting the Facts Straight

This same line of reasoning can be applied to prove the historical accuracy of all the specific events contained in each of the four gospels. If Matthew, Mark, Luke, or John had written of even a *single* event in Jesus' life that didn't actually happen, thousands of first-century people would have immediately recognized their error. And if they could prove one inaccuracy, then the reliability of the entire gospel account would have been rightfully questioned.

For example, what if Jesus hadn't actually raised Lazarus from the dead? If He hadn't, it could have easily been disproved. A person could visit Bethany (Lazarus' hometown), just a few miles from Jerusalem, and conduct an interview *many years* after the supposed incident occurred.

All they had to do was find an elderly person who was around when Lazarus was raised from the dead: "Was there a man named Lazarus who lived here? Did you know him? Did he die? How long was he dead? Did a man named Jesus come to Bethany and raise him from the dead? Were you there when Lazarus came out of his grave? Was he really alive? Did anyone else see it happen? How long did he live after he came back to life?" It wouldn't take long to find out if Jesus really had raised Lazarus.

We know from the Bible account that a *multitude* of people witnessed Lazarus' resurrection (see John 12:17). They weren't just over-zealous followers of Jesus who suffered a mass hallucination either. It was this miracle that convinced the jealous Pharisees that Jesus needed to be killed (see John 11:47-53).

If Jesus hadn't, in fact, raised Lazarus from the dead, then all they had to do was produce the body of Lazarus before the shouting multitude during Jesus' triumphal entry into Jerusalem, and that would have proven Him to be a fake and ended His ministry. But they couldn't deny that Lazarus had indeed convincingly *died* and *come back to life*. The only way they could stop Jesus was to kill Him, and even *that* failed miserably!

So what if Jesus hadn't raised Lazarus from the dead, as the apostle John reports He did? Then you can be sure that John's gospel would never have made it into the second century—much less the twentieth century. Incidentally, we possess a fragment of John's gospel that has been dated 130 A.D.

An author of one of the four gospels couldn't risk reporting *anything* inaccurately. If he made even one mistake, his entire book would have been discredited, as he would have been proven to be an author who could not be trusted. That is why Luke, who wasn't an eyewitness to the events of Jesus' life as were Matthew and John, began his account with the words:

> Inasmuch as many have undertaken to compile an account of the things accomplished among us, just as those who from the beginning were eyewitnesses and servants of the Word [Jesus] have handed them down to us, it seemed fitting for me as well, *having investigated everything carefully from the beginning,* to write it out for you in consecutive order...*so that you may know the exact truth* about the things you have been taught (Luke 1:1-4; italics mine).

The four accounts of Jesus' life have to be accurate, or they wouldn't have survived even one year.

The Accounts Must Be True

If the gospels are not true, then they should be classed in a category far beyond mere myth, fairy tale, or science fiction. Why?

First of all, because of the many *miraculous events* that they record as absolute facts, all of which authenticate Jesus' deity. Second, because of the *words of Jesus*—which the gospel writers claim will determine the eternal destiny of every person, depending on whether or not they are believed.

If the gospel accounts are not true, then they are the most diabolical documents ever penned by men, having led millions into a deception upon which they entrusted their eternal destiny and by which millions wastefully sacrificed their lives.

If the gospels are not accurate historical documents, then their authors are of the most despicable character and should not be revered as saints. Instead, they should be classed beneath the most ignominious figures of history.

You may have heard of Orson Well's radio reading of *The War of the Worlds* on Halloween night in 1938. The drama, thought by many listeners to be an actual news broadcast, resulted in many later-regretted follies by the terrified citizens who prepared for an invasion from Mars.

That deception pales a million-fold in comparison to the damage that has been done by the writing of the gospels, if they are not true. Multitudes of sincere people, down through the centuries, have believed the words of the gospel writers and staked their lives and futures on them. Many have suffered greatly because of their beliefs.

It is impossible, then, to conclude that the gospel accounts can be categorized as harmless myths or fairy tales. The wonders they report as true are too spectacular; the message they contain is too significant.

Either they are part of the most cruel and diabolical conspiracy ever perpetrated, or they are the accurate account of the miracle-working Son of God who became a man. Either you must love the gospels, or you must hate them. But you cannot say they are just another simple myth, like the ones about Pandora or Zeus.

Who Is Jesus?

Because of the historical accuracy of the gospels, we can trust that they contain the actual words that Jesus spoke. And Jesus didn't leave us to second guess who He was. He claimed to be the *divine Son of God*.

Some people are not so foolish as to deny that Jesus was a historical person, yet they prefer to think that Jesus was just a good person—a noble religious leader who taught many wonderful things.

The gospels, however, leave us no option to believe that Jesus was just a good person. One who claims to be the Son of God and the sole source of salvation for all mankind cannot be classified as "just a good man."

Think about it for a moment. Jesus claimed to be the Son of God. He *forgave sins* (Mark 2:5, Luke 7:48), *accepted worship* (Matthew 4:10, 14:33, 28:9), *claimed to be eternal* (John 8:56-58, 17:5), and *presented Himself as the only way to salvation* (John 14:6).

At His trial before the Sanhedrin, the high priest asked Him directly, "Are You the Christ, the Son of the blessed One?" Jesus replied, "I am; and you shall see the Son of Man sitting at the right hand of power, and coming in the clouds of heaven" (Mark 14:61-62).

We can conclude that Jesus was either telling the truth, or He was telling a lie. If He was telling the truth, then He was the divine Son of God. If He was telling a lie about who He was, then either He was doing it consciously, making Himself a cruel deceiver, or else He mistakenly thought He was telling the truth, thus making Himself a lunatic.

So there are our choices. Either Jesus was 1) *God in the flesh;* 2) *an evil, hypocritical liar;* or 3) *He was a crazy-man.* Those are the only options we have. To think He was just a good man—a nice moral teacher—is out of the question.

Every one of us must decide. We can despise Jesus as the worst deceiver who ever lived; we can laugh at Him as a fool with a Messiah-complex; or we can worship Him as God. But we cannot begin to entertain the idea that Jesus was just a good moral teacher.

If He is the Son of God and we believe it, then our lives have to be affected. If we really believe He is the Son of God, then we will want to listen to what He has said and *obey.*

It is impossible to have a casual relationship with Jesus.

§

TEN

The True Mark

I've emphasized again and again in this book that true believers in Jesus are characterized by their unselfish love. They've had their spiritual nature transformed from selfishness to unselfishness.

If a person says he is a Christian but lives entirely for his own selfish ends, he is deceived.

The many selfish acts that have been committed down through the centuries by those who professed Christ serve as irrefutable evidence that those people were *not*, in fact, Christians at all.

The crusaders who waged their "holy wars" and the so-called "servants of Christ" who lavished in extravagant self-indulgence at the expense of the impoverished laity were not born again by God's Spirit. The so-called "Christians" who supported Hitler's "final solution" to exterminate the Jews could not possibly have been true believers in Christ. They may have been "converted" (in their heads), but they'd never been transformed in their hearts and spirits.

We need not travel back in history to find those who profess Christ but deny Him by their actions. The church is full of people *today* who think they are Christians yet who are not. Many who think they are born again are not born again by Christ's Spirit at all.

The Bible gives us a clear standard of measure whereby each of us as individuals can determine if we truly do believe in Jesus. That standard of measure is the love we show to others. That is what this chapter is all about.

If the whole reason we were heading for an eternal hell was because we led lives characterized by selfish ambition, then it would stand to reason that once we enter into a relationship with God we *no longer* lead lives characterized by selfish ambition. That is true repentance.

During His earthly ministry, Jesus disqualified certain individuals from being saved because they demonstrated an unwillingness to repent of their selfish lifestyles.

Yet many churches have preached a watered-down message of salvation, offering it to anyone who will "just accept Jesus" (as if poor Jesus needs our acceptance). These churches, however, fail to inform their congregations of the God-given requirement to turn from selfishness. This watered-down gospel is completely contrary to the gospel of the Bible, as we saw in chapter seven. There is no salvation without repentance; and if a person has truly repented, he has turned from selfishness.

Each of us will be judged by our actions before God. Why? because it is our actions that plainly reveal what is in our hearts. Our deeds do not merit us our salvation, but our deeds *do* prove whether or not we have repented and believed in Jesus. This will become abundantly clear to you as we study what the Bible has to say on the subject.

The Selfish Young Man Jesus Disqualified

Recorded in three out of the four gospels is the very

significant story of a wealthy young man who came to Jesus seeking eternal life. Let's read his story:

> And as He [Jesus] was setting out on a journey, a man ran up to Him and knelt down before Him, and began asking Him, "Good teacher, what shall I do to inherit eternal life?"

> And Jesus said to him, "Why do you call Me good? No one is good except God alone" (Mark 10:17-18).

Already Jesus has made a very significant statement to this young man who desired eternal life. He's told him that all men are sinners because no one is good except God alone. That is the first thing a person needs to know before he can be saved—he must admit he is a sinner.

Second, Jesus has reaffirmed His own deity by implication: He didn't deny that He was, in fact, good, as the young man had said, and then went on to state that only God *is* good. Therefore, He was claiming to be God, which is the second thing a person must believe if he is to be saved.

Let's continue the story as Jesus went on to say:

> "You know the commandments, 'Do not murder, do not commit adultery, do not steal, do not bear false witness, do not defraud, honor your father and mother.'"

> And he said to Him, "Teacher, I have kept all these things from my youth up."

> And looking at him, Jesus felt a love for him, and said to him, "One thing you lack: go and sell all you possess, and give it to the poor, and you shall have treasure in heaven; and come, follow Me." But at these words his face fell, and he went away grieved, for he was one who owned much property.

> And Jesus, looking around, said to His disciples, "How

hard it will be for those who are wealthy to enter the kingdom of God!....It is easier for a camel to go through the eye of a needle than for a rich man to enter the kingdom of God" (Mark 10:19-23, 25).

As you would have expected, Jesus told this young man who was seeking eternal life that he needed to repent and believe in Him— but He didn't use those exact words. After telling the man that all men are sinners and affirming His own deity by implication, Jesus reminded him of the Ten Commandments. In fact, Jesus recited the six commandments that govern man's relationship with his fellowman. The New Testament teaches that God gave the commandments to help us realize how sinful we really are, so we might see our need for a Savior:

Therefore the Law [the Ten Commandments] has become *our tutor to lead us to Christ,* that we might be justified by faith (Galatians 3:24; italics mine).

Jesus wasn't quoting the Ten Commandments so the man would think he could be saved by keeping them, but rather He hoped the man would become acutely aware of how far he'd *fallen short* of keeping them. Then he would see his need for a Savior.

Self-righteously, however, the young man claimed to have kept from his youth the commandments Jesus listed. That just wasn't true, and Jesus was about to prove it to him.

The final commandment Jesus recited to the rich young man was the one that sums up all the commandments governing our relationships with others: *"You shall love your neighbor as yourself."* (Mark's gospel doesn't record Jesus actually reciting this commandment to the man, but Matthew's gospel does; see Matthew 19:16-24.)

This young man was claiming that all of his life he had practiced loving his neighbor as himself. But he really hadn't. How do we know? Because when Jesus told him to sell his possessions and give the money to the poor, the young man wouldn't do it. And why not? The answer is simple: because he would not repent of his selfishness.

Although the rich young man was well aware of the fact that some of his "neighbors" were very poor and needed help, he was unwilling to liquidate any of his assets to assist them. His motivation for living was pure selfish ambition— not service to others. He wouldn't repent, and, thus, couldn't be saved.

Passing the Test

Prior to His conversation with the rich young man, Jesus had already made the profound statement,

> "No one can serve two masters; for either he will hate the one and love the other, or he will hold to one and despise the other. You cannot serve God and mammon [money]" (Matthew 6:24).

In reality, people don't actually serve money. They selfishly serve themselves, and this fact is revealed by what they do with their money. Rather than share it with those who are less fortunate, they hoard it up or spend it on themselves for things they really don't need. But if a person wants to be saved, he must repent of the selfish use of his money.

As John the Baptist boldly proclaimed when people inquired as to what they should do to authenticate their repentance: "Let the man who has two tunics share with him who has none; and let him who has food do likewise" (Luke 3:11).

This is why, as Jesus said, it is so hard for those who are wealthy to enter the kingdom of God. Like everyone else, they must decide if they are going to continue their selfish lifestyle or repent. The rich person's repentance, however, requires paying a higher price. Being saved means he can no longer live in extravagant self-indulgence while, with his full knowledge, multitudes starve.

If God has blessed you with more money than you really need, and if you plan to go to heaven, you will share your blessings with the less fortunate. Again, it's not your good works that will save you, but your works will prove that you have really believed in Jesus. If you continue to selfishly hoard your riches, you are proving to all that you really don't believe in Jesus. Jesus plainly told the rich young ruler that *first* he had to repent of selfishness, and *then* the next step was to follow Him (Jesus).

Does this mean that anyone who wants to be saved must sell all his possessions and give the money to the poor? No. Repentance simply requires a turning from selfishness. To the degree that you've been selfish, to that same degree, you must repent.

If you've been selfish with your money, then you must stop being selfish with it, regardless of how much or how little you possess. Obviously, those who are extremely wealthy and who spend all their money on themselves are going to have to change their lifestyle. True repentance from selfishness may require them to sell some things that are unnecessary, extravagant items and then give the money to those who are less fortunate.

Every person will have to answer to God for himself and satisfy his own conscience. To be saved, we must repent of selfishness, and that means sharing what we have with others.

I'm well aware that what I'm saying isn't popular in our materialistic society and that it flies in the face of what some preachers are saying today. Some even try to convince us that having hundreds of thousands of dollars in the bank and owning extravagant items is a sign of spirituality. That is absurd. Hoarding tons of money is not a sign of spirituality—it's a sign of selfishness.

What if the rich young man had said, "Jesus, I accept you as my Lord and Savior, but I'm going to continue hoarding up more and more money and living for my own selfish desires even though there are so many poor people I could potentially help"? Would that man have been saved? Of course not, as anyone knows who has honestly read the story we just read.

True believers in Jesus are characterized by their unselfish love. And that unselfish love is demonstrated, among other ways, by how they use their money.

Setting the Standard

In the apostle John's first letter, he discusses how it is possible to determine if you are truly a child of God. The determining standard is love, and that love is manifested by actions:

> By this the children of God and the children of the devil are *obvious;* any one who does not practice righteousness is not of God, *nor the one who does not love his brother....*

> We know that we have passed out of death into life [have been born again], *because we love the brethren.* He who does not love abides in death. Everyone who hates his brother is a murderer; and you know that no murderer has eternal life abiding in him.

> We know love by this, that He laid down His life for us; and we ought to lay down our lives for the brethren. *But whoever has the world's goods, and beholds his brother in need and closes his heart against him, how does the love of God abide in him?* Little children, let us not love with word or with tongue, but in deed and in truth... (1 John 3:10, 14-18; italics mine).

That makes it quite plain that the mark of the true Christian is unselfish love, particularly love for his fellow Christian. And that love will be demonstrated not just by words but by actions. That truth is the dominant theme of John's entire first letter.

James, the half-brother of Jesus, wrote a stern letter to the Christians of his day. He told them that they were saved by faith—a faith that was authenticated by acts of unselfish love:

> What use is it, my brethren, if a man says he has faith, but he has no works? Can that faith save him? (James 2:14).

The obvious answer to James' rhetorical question is a resounding, "NO!" Let's continue reading as James illustrates exactly what kind of works he means:

> If a brother or sister is without clothing and in need of daily food, and one of you says to them, "Go in peace, be warmed and be filled," and yet you do not give them what is necessary for their body, what use is that? Even so faith, if it has no works, is dead, being by itself (James 2:15-17).

Once again it is crystal clear that true faith results in deeds of unselfish love.

In a passage in the book of Romans, which I have quoted earlier in this book, the apostle Paul also affirms this same truth:

> But because of your stubbornness and *unrepentant* heart you are storing up wrath for yourself in the day of wrath and revelation of the righteous judgment of God, who will render to every man according to his deeds: to those who by perseverance *in doing good* seek for glory and honor and immortality, *eternal life;* but to those who are *selfishly ambitious* and do not obey the truth, but obey unrighteousness, *wrath and indignation.* There will be tribulation and distress for every soul of man who does evil... (Romans 2:5-9a; italics mine).

These verses have caused embarrassment to some who

have over-emphasized the "faith" requirement of the gospel at the neglect of the "repent" requirement. However, Paul is not saying that we are saved by our works, as is obvious from reading the rest of the book of Romans. He is only reaffirming the truth that true believers have a lifestyle characterized by "doing good," and those whose lives are characterized by selfish ambition are *obviously not* true believers.

Finally, Jesus Himself taught this same truth. We've already witnessed how He required the rich young man to repent of selfishness if he wanted eternal life. In His famous "Sermon on the Mount," Jesus taught His followers to love even their enemies. He said that by so doing, they would prove themselves to be sons of God:

> "And if anyone wants to sue you, and take your shirt, let him have your coat also. And whoever shall force you to go one mile, go with him two. Give to him who asks of you, and do not turn away from him who wants to borrow from you. You have heard that it was said, 'You shall love your neighbor, and hate your enemy.' But I say to you, love your enemies, and pray for those who persecute you, *in order that you may show yourselves to be sons of your Father who is in heaven;* for He causes His sun to rise on the evil and the good, and sends rain on the righteous and the unrighteous.

> "For if you love those who love you, what reward have you? Do not even the tax-gatherers do the same? And if you greet your brothers only, what do you do more than others? Do not even the Gentiles do the same?" (Matthew 5:40-47; italics mine).

Sons of God are supposed to act like God—loving unselfishly. In fact, Jesus said that the mark of His true disciples would be their love for one another:

> "A new commandment I give to you, that you love one

another, even as I have loved you, that you also love one another. By this all men will know that you are my disciples, if you have love for one another" (John 13:34-35).

"You Did It for Me"

The Bible affirms that all of us will be judged according to our deeds—not because our deeds earn us salvation but because our deeds prove whether or not we have truly repented and believed in Jesus. Listen to how Jesus described a certain future judgment before the throne of God:

"But when the Son of Man comes in His glory, and all the angels with Him, then He will sit on His glorious throne. And all the nations will be gathered before Him; and He will separate them from one another, as the shepherd separates the sheep from the goats; and He will put the sheep on His right, and the goats on the left.

"Then the King will say to those on His right, 'Come, you who are blessed of My Father, inherit the kingdom prepared for you from the foundation of the world. For I was hungry, and you gave Me something to eat; I was thirsty, and you gave Me drink; I was a stranger, and you invited Me in; naked, and you clothed Me; I was sick, and you visited Me; I was in prison, and you came to Me.'

"Then the righteous will answer Him, saying, 'Lord, when did we see You hungry, and feed You, or thirsty, and give You a drink? And when did we see You a stranger, and invite You in, or naked, and clothe You? And when did we see You sick, or in prison, and come to You?'

"And the King will answer and say to them, 'Truly I say to you, to the extent that you did it to one of these brothers of Mine, even the least of them, you did it to

Me.'

"Then He will say to those on His left, 'Depart from Me, accursed ones, into the eternal fire which has been prepared for the devil and his angels; for I was hungry, and you gave Me nothing to eat; I was thirsty, and you gave Me nothing to drink; I was a stranger, and you did not invite Me in; naked, and you did not clothe Me, sick, and in prison, and you did not visit Me.'

"Then they themselves will also answer, saying, 'Lord, when did we see You hungry, or thirsty, or a stranger, or naked, or sick, or in prison, and did not serve You?'

"Then He will answer them, saying, 'Truly I say to you, to the extent that you did not do it to one of the least of these, you did not do it to Me.'

"And these will go away into eternal punishment, but the righteous into eternal life" (Matthew 25:31-46).

Those at this judgment will obviously be judged by their deeds. The ones who demonstrated unselfish love will be vindicated as true believers in Jesus. Those who did not demonstrate unselfish love, but rather selfish ambition, will have been proven unbelievers.

In light of all the scriptures I have quoted in this chapter, and in light of the fact that the Bible plainly says that God has deposited His own nature of love within our spirits when we are born again, the truth is obvious: True believers in Jesus will be characterized by unselfish love. And that unselfish love will manifest itself through unselfish deeds and words.

The early church of the apostles obviously understood this truth and practiced it:

And all those who had believed were together, and had all things in common; and they began selling their property and possessions, and were sharing them with all, as anyone might have need....

> And the congregation of those who believed were of one heart and soul; and not one of them claimed that anything belonging to him was his own; but all things were common property to them....
>
> For there was not a needy person among them, for all who were owners of land or houses would sell them and bring the proceeds of the sales, and lay them at the apostles' feet; and they would be distributed to each, as any had need (Acts 2:44-45, 4:32,34-35).

I don't think these first Christians were selling their *primary* homes and giving away the proceeds, or else they would have had nowhere to live themselves. I have to think that those who owned a second home or land they weren't using or unnecessary items sold those things in order to assist the poor. Regardless, the new birth affected how every one of them viewed their possessions. They were no longer private owners, but considered themselves stewards of God's possessions, which were to be shared freely with the other members of His family.

This should be the natural attitude adopted by those who have truly repented of selfishness and believed in Jesus Christ—and not just a phenomena of the "overly-zealous" early Christians. Too many churches, however, are like the church at Ephesus to which Jesus sent the following message:

> "But I have this against you, that you have left your first love. Remember therefore from where you have fallen, and repent and do the deeds you did at first..." (Revelation 2:4-5a).

Bible interpreters have argued concerning what exactly was the "first love" that the Ephesians left. Was it daily Bible reading? Was it devotion to prayer? Was it attending church?

My opinion is that Jesus was referring to none of those things. I think He meant exactly what He said, that they had left their first love—that is, that they weren't demonstrating the love toward others they'd demonstrated at first. And that is why Jesus told them to repent and do the deeds they'd done originally.

Three Things You Need to Know

My reason for writing this chapter is three-fold.

First of all, I realize that some people have avoided the message of the gospel because they have experienced the hatred of some *so-called* Christians. I wanted those unfortunate people to understand that the so-called Christians who hated them were not, in fact, true Christians at all. My hope is that now they will consider the words of Jesus, repent of their own sins, and believe in Him.

Second, I wanted every Christian reader to look within himself and perform a personal spiritual diagnosis to determine whether his profession of faith is genuine. Hopefully, some who have been motivated solely by selfish ambition, and yet thought they were born again, now realize their self-deception. I pray they have now truly repented and believed in Jesus.

May I also add that all Christians are daily tempted to act selfishly, and none of us has reached perfection in unselfish love. That is what we are striving for. The Bible makes it plain that love is a fruit that should be growing continually in the life of every believer (see Galatians 5:22, 1 Thessalonians 3:12-13, 1 John 2:5, 4:12, 17-18).

Just because we yield to the temptation to commit some small selfish act does not mean we are not really saved. When a true Christian does commit an act of selfishness, he will feel guilty in his spirit and should immediately ask for God's forgiveness. God, of course, will grant it to him (see I John 1:9). Still, the Bible teaches that our hearts can be assured that we truly are saved as we love unselfishly (see 1 John 3:16-21, 4:16-18).

And *third*, I wrote this chapter so that Christians might stop and question how non-Christians view them. Are we presenting a true representation of Christ to the world? Are we communicating a message to non-Christians that we love them as God loves them?

Why is it that, so often, unbelievers think that born-again people are only a bunch of self-righteous moralists who are zealous for conservative political causes? Why don't they speak of us as the ones who are always serving others, who are full of mercy when wronged, who pray for those who hate them, who generously share their belongings, and who love all men, regardless of their social status, their race, their religion, or their conduct?

Oh, how more of us need to live up to our label: "Christian," which means "Christ-like"!

§

"Therefore be imitators of God, as beloved children; and walk in love, just as Christ also loved you, and gave Himself up for us, an offering and a sacrifice to God..." (Ephesians 5:1-2).

ELEVEN

What Next?

S o now you are a new believer in Jesus Christ. Happy Spiritual Birthday!

What do you do now? Of course, your entire motivation for living has been radically changed from selfishness to self*less*ness.

Is there anything else you should begin doing? Yes.

In God's eyes, you are a brand-new spiritual baby, and He wants you to grow up—spiritually. He wants you to become like Jesus. That will take years. It will require effort on your part.

In this short chapter, I want to share with you what you should do to begin your spiritual journey. Keep in mind that our goal, of course, is to become like Jesus.

Reading the Bible

Obviously, if you want to become like Jesus, you'll have to get to know Him. There are four records of His life, called the *Gospels*, contained in the New Testament. Written by Matthew, Mark, Luke, and John, each author tells Jesus' story from a little different perspective, so you need to read them all.

After the gospels, the book of Acts tells about the early Church, its leaders, and the spread of the gospel.

Next you'll find a collection of letters written to the early Christians by Paul, James, Peter, John, and Jude. All of these men were inspired by the Holy Spirit to write their letters. That means you can read them as personal love-letters from God.

You should read those letters after you've finished the four gospels. It's important to read the New Testament before you begin reading the Old Testament. The New Testament was written for Christians—people who are living under the new covenant (or promises) that Jesus inaugurated. You are living under that new covenant with God.

I can guarantee you that you won't understand everything you read in the Bible the first time, but don't worry about it— just apply what you *do* understand. The more you read and study the Bible, the more you'll learn. The Bible is such an amazing book that you can read it over and over a thousand times and still won't know all there is to know.

I encourage you to read a portion of the Bible every day. If you want some help in understanding it, I've written another book entitled *Your Best Year Yet* (Creation House). It follows a daily reading program that guides you through the entire Bible in one year and contains a commentary on every day's reading. You can get a copy at any Christian bookstore or by using the order form at the end of this book.

Finding a Church

You will also need to attend a church regularly where the Bible is faithfully preached. Unfortunately, the true gospel is not preached in all churches, so you need to be careful.

How can you find a good church to attend? First of all, ask the person who gave you this book. Chances are, he or she is born again and attends a church where the Bible is preached.

When you are in a church where the people are born again, they are warm and friendly. If you feel unwelcome, you're not among true Christians. Keep looking. Make certain the church you attend is full of *true Christians* not just religious people who think they are Christians.

God will also use other Christians to help you to grow spiritually. They are your older brothers and sisters, spiritually speaking. That is another way to tell if you are in a church where the people really understand the gospel—many times they refer to one another as their fellow "brothers and sisters in Christ."

Another way to determine if you are in a good church is to ask the pastor if he agrees with the message contained in this book! If a pastor doesn't agree with the fundamental message of Jesus' death on the cross for the propitiation of our sins and that we are saved through repentance and faith in Jesus, then that pastor needs to be saved himself.

There are many different viewpoints concerning minor doctrinal matters among churches and ministers, but all true Christians agree on the basic Bible gospel. If the pastor doesn't believe the simple gospel message, find one who does.

A God-called pastor is specially equipped with certain gifts that enable him to help you grow. You definitely need to place yourself under the care of a loving, Bible-preaching pastor. He is a gift from God to you.

Being Baptized in Water

Ask your new pastor to baptize you in water as soon as possible. Jesus said, "He who has believed and has been baptized shall be saved; but he who has disbelieved shall be condemned" (Mark 16:16). Of course, being baptized doesn't

119

save you, but it is one of the first things that authenticates your true repentance and faith.

If your pastor says that it is not important to be baptized, keep looking for a good church. Chances are if a pastor doesn't obey the clear and simple commandment to baptize new Christians, he won't be following the Bible in a lot of other areas as well.

You may have been baptized as a baby in a church, or maybe you weren't, but it doesn't make any difference. The Bible teaches that everyone should be baptized *after* he professes faith in Jesus Christ as his Savior. Your infant baptism had nothing to do with your own personal acceptance of Jesus.

Why is water baptism so important? Because it is symbolic of what happened to Jesus, and through baptism, we are identifying with Him. Christ Jesus died, was buried, and was raised from the dead for our salvation. So we too, in baptism, have died, been buried (under the water), and been raised as new persons, washed clean from sin!

Sharing the Gospel

You have no doubt already felt the urge to tell others about what you have learned. You know that if they don't repent and believe the gospel, they are going to spend eternity in hell. God's love in you is what causes that compassion for unsaved people to well up in your heart.

I recommend that you go slowly as you begin to share your new-found faith with others. I say that because I made many mistakes when I first began "witnessing" to my unsaved friends. Usually I wound up arguing about minor doctrinal points of their particular church's creed rather than effectively communicating the simple gospel of God's love expressed through Jesus' sacrifice.

To make matters worse, I came across as a know-it-all and realize now that I was too pushy with my potential converts.

So I'm recommending that you begin by *praying* on a daily basis for your friends and relatives who aren't yet saved.

Before you tell them about the change that has happened in your life, you need to *demonstrate* a changed life. When they notice the change and begin asking you what has happened, then it's a good time to gently and respectfully tell them what God has done for you (see 1 Peter 3:15-16). If they laugh, don't retaliate or criticize their particular beliefs. Forgive them, continue to pray for them, and look for opportunities where you can serve them. Love can melt a hardened heart.

Be careful that you don't unconsciously portray a "holier-than-thou" attitude to those who are unsaved. Obviously, you won't be participating any longer in the sinful practices of those who don't believe in Jesus, but you must take precaution lest others think that you imagine yourself to be better than they are. Don't ever forget that you once acted just as they do and that it's only because you heard the gospel and responded that you no longer live a life of sin. We are saved only because of God's mercy, so we certainly have no right to be proud.

If you spend a lot of time with *unreceptive* unbelievers, they will drag you down spiritually. That is another reason why you need to be fellowshipping with other Christians regularly and not *just* in church. As you grow spiritually, your closest friends will become those who are part of your spiritual family—the family of God.

Prayer

Because God is now your Father, you will want to develop your Father-child relationship with Him. You don't have to be in church to talk with Him because He's *with* you and *in* you all the time by the Holy Spirit. He wants you to enjoy fellowship with Him all day long.

You should talk to God about everything. You don't need

to use "Thee's" and "Thou's." Just talk to Him as you would talk to your father because He is your Father. When you pray and ask Him for something, make certain that what you are asking for is in His will, based upon a promise you've found in the Bible. Then you can pray with faith, certain that God will give you your request.

The apostle John wrote:

> And this is the confidence which we have before Him, that, if we ask anything according to His will, He hears us. And if we know that He hears us in whatever we ask, we know that we have the requests which we have asked from Him (1 John 5:14-15).

As you mature spiritually, you will eventually learn to hear God speaking to you. It will take some time to discern God's voice. Now you are just a newborn spiritual baby, and a newborn baby has no idea what his parents are saying to him. Don't expect to hear an audible voice or even words that come from inside you. God speaks to us through impressions within us, and it takes continued, meditative prayer to discern those impressions.

For now, you should only concern yourself with hearing from God through His written Word, the Bible. That is the primary way God speaks to us. As you continue to grow spiritually, then you can begin to practice listening to God as He speaks to you by the Holy Spirit within you.

If you ever think that God has spoken to you to do something that contradicts what He has already said in the written Word, you are mistaken because God never contradicts Himself.

What if I Sin?

Once you repent and accept Christ as your Savior, does that mean from then on you will be living a life of sinless perfection? No. Because when you first repent, you'll only be able to repent of the selfish acts of which you are conscious.

As you continue growing spiritually, God will reveal further areas of your life that need repentance. That is the process which is referred to in the Bible as *sanctification.* Sanctification is a progressive work in your life.

The Bible makes it plain that Christians are tempted and that they sometimes sin. Thankfully the sacrificial death of Christ covers those sins as well!

What can we do if we sin after our initial repentance? The apostle John told us how to deal with sin in our lives:

> And if anyone sins, we have an Advocate with the Father, Jesus Christ the righteous; and He Himself is the propitiation for our sins; and not for ours only, but also for those of the whole world.
>
> If we *confess* our sins, He is faithful and righteous to *forgive* us our sins and to *cleanse* us from all unrighteousness (1 John 2:1b-2, 1:9; italics mine).

Once we confess our sins, they are forgiven by God, by means of Jesus' death. The Christian will discover that he will *always* need Jesus to be his Savior from his sins.

And Finally...

If you have been born again through reading this book, would you be so kind to write a short note and tell me? I would greatly appreciate it, and it would fill me with joy to hear of another person who has become a member of God's world-wide family. You can write me at: P.O. Box 0446, Library, PA 15129. Thanks! I look forward to hearing from you!

§

TWELVE

The Future
is Ours to See

Why did God go to all this trouble to save us from sin, death, and hell?

Surely the all-knowing, all-wise God, the Creator of our incredibly complex and still mysterious universe, the Designer of all living things, the One who has existed from eternity has a reason for having created us. There must be some ultimate goal that God has been working toward— something He's had in mind for a long, long time.

The Bible plainly states that before the creation of the world God formulated a plan.

That plan involves you and me.

God planned to have a big family, filled with His love, whom He could enjoy and who would enjoy Him. They would live together forever in a perfect society and a perfect world. You can call it heaven; you can call it utopia; you can call it paradise—it doesn't matter. But some day, all of us who have believed in Jesus will be there.

So why didn't God just start things off that way? Why haven't we been experiencing that perfect world all along?

God did start things off that way—in the Garden of Eden with a perfectly beautiful paradise filled with everything man needed to live a happy and fulfilling life. What happened? The people God created refused to cooperate with His plan.

But that hasn't stopped God from planning. In spite of what people have done, God's dream *will* be fulfilled.

The Test of Love

Why, then, didn't God create people who *would* cooperate? Now that is an easy question to answer. If God had created us all as robots, programmed to obey, with no freedom to choose to disobey, then He could never have had a family who loved Him or who loved one another.

The foundation of love is free choice.

What makes my relationship with my wife so wonderful is that she didn't *have* to marry me, but she did. She chose to be my wife, and she chooses to continue to be my wife. And *that is love*. If there is no choice in that matter, there is no love.

How would God have felt with a race of robots? I'll give you an idea.

Sometime when you are feeling lonely, take a tape recorder and record your own voice saying, "I love you. You are a wonderful person. Oh, how I enjoy being with you. Your conversation is so interesting. Your jokes are so funny. I'm so lucky to have you as my friend."

Then rewind the tape, fix yourself a cup of tea, and sit down and listen to what you've just recorded. Will hearing it give you a warm feeling down in your heart? Will you pull down the shades and hold that tape recorder close to your heart? Will you promise never to leave that tape recorder, to nurse it when its batteries get low, never to glance at a newer model in the Sears Catalogue?

Do you see what I'm getting at? What makes love so

beautiful is that even though there was an option *not* to love, the choice was made to love. God didn't want a family of robots anymore than you want an inflatable wife or husband.

When God granted the creatures who were created in His image the privilege of free moral agency, He took a risk—by human standards that is. He risked the fact that some would choose *not* to love Him, and, therefore, would not obey Him. But there was no other alternative.

If You are God, and You want a family that loves You, then You must create people who can chose *not* to love You.

In a simple sense, that is the purpose of this present life. It serves as a test for every person: first of all, to see if each one will chose to love or hate God. It is easy to tell who loves Him and who hates Him. How? By whether or not they *obey* Him.

Of course, every person has initially chosen *not* to obey God, but God has mercifully given him a second chance, and done it justly by means of the sacrifice of His Son Jesus. You already know all about that.

Some people will no doubt say, "I love God, but I'll never become a Christian."

But Jesus said, "If you love Me, you will keep My commandments" (John 14:15). It's just that simple. People who say they love God, but who don't do what Jesus says, are fooling themselves.

Eventually, the timer-bell rings, and each person's test is over. Then the grades are passed out at the judgment seat of God. There is no second chance after that. If you haven't decided to stop serving yourself and chosen to begin serving God in seventy or so years, you wouldn't change if you had seven *thousand* years. God can't wait forever; He wants to get on with His plan.

It's a fact that the older an unsaved person grows, the more *unlikely* he is to repent and believe in Jesus.

My seven-year old daughter once said to me (after she had shared about Jesus with one of her little neighbor-friends),

127

"Daddy, little kids are easy to make into Christians. Teenagers are a lot harder. And grown-ups are *really* hard." What she said has been proven statistically.

Foreknown but Not Foredone

God has known from eternity past who would choose to repent and believe in Jesus and who would not. The Bible says that our names have been written in a book called *the Lamb's book of life* "from the foundation of the world" (see Revelation 13:8, 17:8). If you have just become one of God's children, He knew it was going to happen ages ago.

So, you might ask, if God knew who would choose to serve Him, then why didn't He create everyone at once, take the ones He knew would serve Him to heaven, and send the ones to hell whom He knew wouldn't serve Him?

The answer is that God only foreknows the outcome of each individual's test once he has actually experienced a test. Only that which is known could potentially have been foreknown. Let me give you an example.

Suppose you suddenly found yourself possessing a gift to know in advance the outcome of every football game. Wouldn't that be wonderful? Let's say that you correctly predicted the outcome of every professional football game this year, and it was documented by the highest authorities.

Then let's imagine that someone makes the suggestion, "Hey, why should we go to all the trouble to play the games anymore? Why risk the players being injured? Why expend all that effort? Let's stop playing football games and just let our friend here, who is never wrong, tell us in advance the outcomes of the games that would have been played!" And let's say that everyone agreed it was a good plan, and all football games that season were cancelled.

Then, on national television, instead of the first football game, a camera is pointed at you, and the sports announcer asks, "Okay, since you always have the ability to know the outcome of every football game before it is played, who would have won this football game today?"

What will you say? You will say, "I don't know. In order for me to foreknow who will win, the game must be played at some point in time, or else there is nothing for me to foreknow."

Can you see it? The game must be played so that a winner is determined. Then there is something to know about who won and lost. And then, if you have the ability, there is something to foreknow.

Out of Time

It is difficult for us to comprehend the fact that God does not live in the realm of time. He has no beginning and no end, and, therefore, time is not of His realm. The only way to remotely imagine His realm is to view a fold-out time-line from a history book.

On that time-line, you can see the age of the dinosaurs, the burning of Rome, and the landing of the first man on the moon. But imagine a little ant walking on that time-line. At any given moment, he can only see one event as he travels the line. Yet from your perspective, you can see it all.

That is somewhat how God sees things. He knows the end from the beginning. To Him, all is *right now*. What we call history, or the future, to God is now.

People sometimes ask, "How will God be able to judge every individual person? That would take years and years. Will we have to stand in line for centuries waiting our turn?" They are speaking from a time orientation.

God has all eternity to judge everyone, but it will take no time at all because there will be no time. That is also why we'll all be able to enjoy His personal fellowship for eternity. You'll be able to spend as much time with God as you like, and so will everyone else, because there won't be any time to think about.

Now, back to our time-line. Certainly, ten thousand years ago, God could have looked down the eons of time to your life and seen how you reacted to your test. (Which He did and wrote down what He saw.) But unless you are tested at some point in time, there would be nothing for God to look at down through time and see!

It is at the time of your test that the knowledge of whether you passed or failed became available to God to know, and, thus, to foreknow. That is why He didn't create everyone all at once and bring the ones He knew would serve Him immediately to heaven and send the rest to hell.

For us, time is running out, literally, and will one day stop forever. But you can see that from God's standpoint, His plan has already been fully consummated. That is why, many times in the Bible, the future is described as if it had already happened. Sometimes, God allowed His prophets to see things happening that are yet to happen (from our perspective).

The New Earth

One of those fortunate people who saw into the future was the apostle John. God let him see the new earth of the future as it was freshly recreated. That will be the time when, as far as we presently know, God's plan will be fully consummated, and time will stop. Let me quote to you John's description of what he saw and comment as we go:

> And I saw a new heaven and a new earth; for the first heaven and the first earth passed away, and there is no longer any sea (Revelation 21:1).

This shouldn't surprise us because Jesus promised that "heaven and earth will pass away" (Matthew 24:35). I assume that the heaven to which He and John referred is not the heaven where God presently lives but the atmospheric heaven. There won't be any air pollution then!

John also said there would no longer be any sea. That doesn't mean there won't be any lakes or ponds—just no oceans.

> And I saw the holy city, new Jerusalem, coming down out of heaven from God, made ready as a bride adorned for her husband. And I heard a voice saying, "Behold, the tabernacle of God is among men, and He shall dwell among them, and they shall be His people, and God Himself will be among them, and He shall wipe away every tear from their eyes; and there shall no longer be any death; there shall no longer be any mourning, or crying, or pain; the first things have passed away" (Revelation 21:2-4).

This "New Jerusalem" that John saw, according to other scriptures, is presently in heaven. Again, this shouldn't surprise us, as Jesus promised us He would go to heaven and prepare a place for us:

> "Let not your heart be troubled; believe in God, believe also in Me. In My Father's house are many dwelling places; if it were not so, I would have told you; for I go to prepare a place for you" (John 14:1-2).

So we know that one of the things Jesus has been doing for the past 2,000 years is working on preparing a place for you and me in God's house—probably located somewhere in the New Jerusalem.

In that city, there won't be any coffin-makers or undertakers in the yellow pages! Neither will there be any sorrow or pain. I can't comprehend that, but I can believe it and anticipate it!

> And He who sits on the throne said, "Behold, I am making all things new." And He said, "Write, for these words are faithful and true." And He said to me, "It is done. I am the Alpha and Omega, the beginning and the

131

end. I will give to the one who thirsts from the spring of the water of life without cost. He who overcomes shall inherit these things, and I will be his God and he will be My son" (Revelation 21:5-7).

Anyone who is spiritually thirsty qualifies to drink freely from the spring of the water of life. There is a literal spring of the water of life in the New Jerusalem, but this statement also applies to the Christian's new birth. It is just one more way of saying that anyone can be saved, pass from spiritual death to spiritual life, and be born again. Notice it is free, unmerited and undeserved, and offered to all. Those who drink will become God's sons. And what will become of those who refuse to drink?

> But for the cowardly and unbelieving and abominable persons and sorcerers and idolaters and all liars, *their part will be in the lake that burns with fire and brimstone,* which is the second death (Revelation 21:8; italics mine).

Praise God that we don't have to fear spending eternity in that terrible lake of fire.

Our Future Home

As John's vision progressed, he was given a closer look at the New Jerusalem, our future home:

> And he [an angel] carried me away in the Spirit to a great and high mountain, and showed me the holy city, Jerusalem, coming down out of heaven from God, having the glory of God. Her brilliance was like a very costly stone, as a stone of jasper. It had a great and high wall, with twelve gates, and at the gates twelve angels....

> And the one who spoke with me had a gold measuring rod to measure the city, and its gates and its wall. And the

city is laid out as a square, and its length is as great as the width; and he measured the city with the rod, fifteen hundred miles; its length and width and height are equal (Revelation 21:10-12a, 15-16).

This is a big city! It would cover more than one-half the surface of the United States! And it is 1,500 miles high, being either a gigantic cube or a triangle!

And the material of the wall was jasper; and the city was pure gold, like clear glass....And the twelve gates were twelve pearls; each one of the gates was a single pearl. And the street of the city was pure gold, like transparent glass (Revelation 21:18, 21).

God obviously spared no expense when He built this city. There won't be any need for road-repair crews!

And I saw no temple in it, for the Lord God, the Almighty, and the Lamb, are its temple. And the city had no need of the sun or of the moon to shine upon it, for the glory of God has illumined it, and its lamp is the Lamb (Revelation 21:22-23).

That doesn't necessarily mean that there won't be any sun or moon in heaven. But this city won't need them because the glory that radiates from the Father and the Son will shine through the entire city—right through the walls of transparent gold. Can you imagine how it will look?

God once allowed three men, Peter, James, and John to see Jesus as He will appear in His glorified state. Jesus had told them they would soon see Him as He will look in His kingdom, and six days later they did:

And He [Jesus] was transfigured before them; and His face shone like the sun, and His garments became as white as light (Matthew 17:2).

Mark, in his gospel, described Jesus' garments as becoming "radiant and exceedingly white, as no launderer on earth can whiten them" (Mark 9:3). Luke stated that Jesus' clothing "became white and flashing like lightening" (Luke 9:29). Someday you'll see Him just as Peter, James, and John did!

What Will We Do in Heaven?

Let's continue reading John's account of the New Jerusalem:

> And the nations shall walk by its light, and the kings of the earth shall bring their glory into it. And in the daytime (for there shall be no night there) its gates shall never be closed; and they shall bring the glory and the honor of the nations into it; and nothing unclean and no one who practices abomination and lying, shall ever come into it, but only those whose names are written in the Lamb's book of life (Revelation 21:24-27).

So there will be kings living on the new earth who will visit the capital of the world and do homage to God and His Son who reside there. No one who is a liar will enter there—which all of us were until we were born again. *Liars aren't born again.*

> And he showed me a river of the water of life, clear as crystal, coming from the throne of God and of the Lamb, in the middle of its street. And on either side of the river was the tree of life, bearing twelve kinds of fruit, yielding its fruit every month; and the leaves of the tree were for the healing of the nations.

> And there shall no longer be any curse; and the throne of God and of the Lamb shall be in it, and His bond-servants shall serve Him; and they shall see His face, and His name shall be on their foreheads.

> And there shall no longer be any night; and they shall not

have need of the light of a lamp nor the light of the sun, because the Lord God shall illumine them; and they shall reign forever and ever (Rev. 22:1-5).

Who fully understands all that these verses are saying? No one, but some day we all will.

Maybe you've wondered: What will we be doing all through eternity? At least two things: We will be *serving God* and *reigning*. As Jesus promised, "Blessed are the gentle, for they shall inherit the earth" (Matthew 5:5). He meant that literally!

Heaven will be a place of unimaginable beauty and unimaginable peace, joy, and love. *It will be the place that God planned for us ages ago.*

Heaven's Friendships

There is more I could say on this subject of heaven, but let me interject one more thought from Scripture.

Jesus said that in heaven there will be no marriage (see Matthew 22:30). That is why, in our vows, we say "till death do us part." The idea of no marriage in heaven may not sound so good to those of us on earth, especially if we're enjoying the blessings of a Christian marriage.

We can safely conclude, however, that God has a good reason for leaving marriage out of heaven. There must be something better to replace it.

Could it be that the love and transparency that we can only experience within marriage on earth is something that we will experience with everyone in heaven? Everyone will be "best friends"! Think about that!

Last Words

If I don't have the opportunity to be your friend on earth, then I'm looking forward to being your friend in heaven. We'll have to get together for a thousand years and get to know each other! See you then!

Also by David Kirkwood...

Your Best Year Yet is a daily devotional-commentary that will help you read through the entire Bible in one year. This easy-to-read devotional follows the reading plan of the *One Year Bible*®, and contains inspirational reflections, historical background notes, and life-changing applications for each day's reading from the Old and New Testaments. Discover fresh insights from God's Word to help make this year...*Your Best Year Yet*! Available at your local Christian bookstore or by using the order form below. (ISBN 0-88419-274-1, 480 pages, Trade paper, $15.95)

You can also order additional copies of *Forgive Me For Waiting so Long to Tell You This* by using the order form below, or save postage and handling costs and order from your local Christian bookstore.

Book Title	No. of copies	Price	Extended Price
Forgive Me For Waiting so Long to Tell You This		$6.95	
Your Best Year Yet		$15.95	
If ordering less than 5 books, add $2.00 shipping and handling per book		$2.00	
If ordering 5 or more books, add $1.00 shipping and handling per book		$1.00	
Total Amount Enclosed			

Send order form and payment to: **ETHNOS Press, P.O. Box 0446, Library, PA 15129**

Also by David Kirkwood...

Your Best Year Yet is a daily devotional-commentary that will help you read through the entire Bible in one year. This easy-to-read devotional follows the reading plan of the *One Year Bible*®, and contains inspirational reflections, historical background notes, and life-changing applications for each day's reading from the Old and New Testaments. Discover fresh insights from God's Word to help make this year...*Your Best Year Yet*! Available at your local Christian bookstore or by using the order form below. (ISBN 0-88419-274-1, 480 pages, Trade paper, $15.95)

You can also order additional copies of *Forgive Me For Waiting so Long to Tell You This* by using the order form below, or save postage and handling costs and order from your local Christian bookstore.

Book Title	No. of copies	Price	Extended Price
Forgive Me For Waiting so Long to Tell You This		$6.95	
Your Best Year Yet		$15.95	
If ordering less than 5 books, add $2.00 shipping and handling per book		$2.00	
If ordering 5 or more books, add $1.00 shipping and handling per book		$1.00	
Total Amount Enclosed			

Send order form and payment to: **ETHNOS Press, P.O. Box 0446, Library, PA 15129**

DATE DUE